MW00364918

There Is Hope

There Is Hope

Laura Lee and Doug Oldham

Fleming H. Revell
A Division of Baker Book House Co
Grand Rapids, Michigan 49516

Published by Fleming H. Revell
a division of Baker Book House Company
P.O. Box 6287, Grand Rapids, MI 49516-6287

Printed in the United States of America

Library of Congress Cataloging-in-Publication Data

Oldham, Laura Lee, 1931–
    There is hope / Laura Lee and Doug Oldham.
    p. cm.
    ISBN 0-8007-1727-9 (cloth)
    1. Oldham, Laura Lee, 1931– . 2. Oldham, Doug. 3. Christian biography—United States. 4. Gospel musicians—United States—Biography. 5. Married people—Religious life. 6. Marriage—Religious aspects—Christianity. I. Oldham, Doug. II. Title.
BR1700.2.053 1996
248.8′44′0922—dc20
[B]   96-21553

Contents

Contents

Acknowledgments

This book is dedicated to our family:

Daughters Paula, Karen, and Dee
Sons-in-law John E. Johnson and Buz Offenbacker
Grandchildren Jamaica, John Jr., Jessy, and Nathan

Special thank-you's go to:

Clare Pharais, longtime friend who said "There's a book here" as he read our writings

Mark Gough, editor, who first requested the book for his company

Rich Baker, of Baker Books, for accepting the book

Bill Petersen, editor, for his wonderful, genuine Christian spirit in dealing with us

Dave Wimbish, for organizing and shaping the manuscript into its final form

The many typists, in all parts of the country, who typed and typed, some of whom include Debbie VanBrackle, Linda Page, and Jay Hart, all of Lynchburg, Virginia; Barbara Wright, Ann Mardis, and Leona Crain, all of Campbellville, Kentucky; and Sally Jo Harshman of Lake Wales, Florida

Rose Marie Owens, who finally retyped the entire manuscript and put it all on a computer disk

Ruth and Elmer Towns, who pitched our writings to another company and encouraged us to "press on toward the goal"

Those who took the family photographs, including Jonathan Falwell, John E. Johnson, Dee Oldham, and Doug Oldham

Part One

*A Marriage
in Trouble*

From the top:
Laura Lee and Doug
Paula and John Johnson
Karen and Gary (Buz) Offenbacker
Granddaughter Jessy

The Wedding Dress

For He has clothed me with garments of salvation,
He has wrapped me with a robe of righteousness,
As a bridegroom decks himself with a garland,
And as a bride adorns herself with her jewels. . . .
So the Lord God will cause righteousness and praise
To spring up before all nations.

Isaiah 61:10–11 NASB

Laura Lee:

It was Christmas week and my heart was singing.

The "clan" had gathered in! The children and grandchildren were home—it was every mother's dream of a perfect Christmas. Not only do people come to our clan gatherings, the dogs and cats come too. It adds to the noise and the excitement, don't you know!

Dee, our youngest daughter, had made it through the snow from Nashville with her old English sheepdog, Gracie, and her rag doll cat, Georgia.

Karen, our middle child, had come in from New Jersey bringing Jessy and Nathan. Buz, her husband, couldn't come because of church work, so he got to keep their golden retriever.

Paula, our oldest, and her husband, John, came across town with John Jr. and Jamaica, and Smokey, the toy poodle.

Add Doug and me and our two dogs and a cat and, violà, you have the "clan."

I was a happy camper because they were home.

I was baking raisin cookies and they smelled wonderful. The sounds of everybody laughing and talking filled the air. I started out of the kitchen to check the fire in the living room fireplace and stopped dead in my tracks.

Coming shyly, tentatively into the room through the opposite doorway was thirteen-year-old Jessy. She was wearing my wedding dress.

She stopped by the Christmas tree with a little, pleased smile on her gorgeous, innocent face. Her long, thick, dark hair with its one natural light streak fell around her shoulders. As she looked at me with her blue eyes, I could plainly see the young dreams that were tucked away inside her heart.

The live, green Christmas tree was decorated with white doves, white flowers, and white lights. The forty-four-year-old white satin dress shone in the light of the tree and the fire. It was a moment frozen in time.

There was that dress. There it was again!

It is a dress that in a funny way has defined all our lives. It is a dress that one day symbolized my young, innocent dreams, then ended up almost discarded, just like my marriage. But the dress was reclaimed, as was the marriage, and it was worn with joy by . . . But I'm getting ahead of the story. Let me tell you about the dress.

I didn't like it much when I first saw it, but it was cheap. It had been on display in the window of the little store, and it was just my size. So I put a little money down and promised that I'd be back with another fifty dollars, which I had no idea how I was going to get.

My in-laws-to-be were graciously paying for the church wedding, but I felt obligated to at least pay for my own gown, although that wasn't going to be easy. Doug and I were both college students, and it was all I could do to scrape together enough money for books and tuition. Fifty dollars might as well have been five hundred as far as I was concerned.

But within two weeks, a plain white envelope arrived in the college mail. There was no return address. When I opened it, I was stunned to find a cashier's check in the amount of fifty dollars. I had no way of knowing who had sent the money, although I suspected that it might be the mutual friend who was serving as Doug's best man. When I asked him about it, he only smiled a rather mysterious smile and said he didn't know anything about it.

He sure looked guilty to me.

After the wedding, the dress was boxed and moved with all our other things so many times I sort of lost track of it. It had served its purpose and didn't seem to be of any other use to me.

Then one day a few weeks before her wedding, Paula, our oldest daughter, came sailing down the stairs with my wedding dress on, laughing and dancing and saying to her excited sisters and girlfriend, "Oh, I found it! I love it! I'm going to wear it for my wedding!"

I was aghast!

"Why?" I asked. "That's a terrible wedding dress. I never liked it."

"Oh no, it's not!" she contradicted me. "It's beautiful and I'm going to wear it!"

And she did.

And you know what? She was right. It was beautiful, or, more correctly, she was beautiful wearing it.

She also wore a lovely lace veil that we had purchased from a saleslady who kept insisting that "it's really out of style" and that "no one wants it." We had to practically beg her to let us buy it, but she finally reluctantly agreed, and it went with the dress perfectly.

After the wedding, the dress was packed away again—only with much more care this time.

And then came the time for daughter Karen to walk down the aisle.

"I'll wear the dress too, Mama, and I'll wear Paula's veil! I love it. It will be so beautiful!"

A friend of hers made a trip to Chicago where she bought some fabulous imported lace that looked very much like the lace on the veil. Then she cut out lace flowers and appliquéd them all over the soft, old, satin dress. It was suddenly lovely enough to be in a museum.

When Karen came down the aisle wearing my dress and her sister's veil, she looked so gorgeous that I thought my heart would stop.

I could scarcely believe how beautiful that dress was—the dress that I didn't really like and had bought cheap and had hauled around not paying it any mind, considering it worthless. There it was, looking for all the world like a royal robe fit for a queen.

What of its value now? Priceless. Absolutely priceless.

And not because of the satin, the lace, or the style. Priceless because my two lovely daughters had loved me so much that they wanted to wear my dress on their wedding days.

And priceless because my own marriage had come back from the brink of divorce—not only come back, but come back with great love and beauty. Priceless because of two more young marriages doing well. And priceless because my daughters and I both said our vows standing before my father-in-law, the girls' grandfather, who performed all three weddings.

Those are just some of the reasons why a piece of satin and lace can be called priceless.

And by the way, remember the cashier's check that had paid for the dress in the first place? I found out something very interesting on our twenty-fifth wedding anniversary.

We were at Longfellows Wayside Inn near Boston with friends Joe and Judy Moscheo. We had just gone on a sleigh ride in an old-fashioned sleigh pulled by horses. Our anniversary dinner was being served in the old kitchen near the fireplace. We were laughing and talking.

Doug said, "Laura Lee, did you ever find out who sent you the money to pay for your wedding dress?"

I answered, "No, I never did."

He said, "I guess it's safe after all this time to tell you. I did."

Yes, some things are definitely priceless.

I had met Doug Oldham when we were both students at a Christian college. In spite of our differences, I was attracted to him right from the start—and those differences were not slight.

Doug grew up in a parsonage, an only child, trained in the church. He was singing in church and camp meetings from the time he was in junior high school. His father was a leader and preacher of great worth, known far and wide in the denomination.

Me? I was a mountain girl with no worldly props around me. I had not grown up in the church, but came to know Jesus as a teenager and made up my mind that I would do what I could to serve him. I decided I would go to a Christian college. My family objected, but I left anyway, traveling all the way from Nebraska to Indiana with eighty dollars in my pocket. I had no job and knew no one, but I felt secure in my relationship with God. I knew he would see me through . . . and he did.

Soon after my arrival in Indiana I met Doug. And soon after that I was dreaming the kind of dreams that I saw in Jessy's eyes when she tried on the wedding dress.

Sometimes it takes a while for the "good" dreams to come true. I'll let Doug tell you about what happened in the meantime.

How I Played
the Numbers Game and Lost

For I have the desire to do what is good, but I cannot carry it out. For what I do is not the good I want to do; no, the evil I do not want to do—this I keep on doing.

Romans 7:18–19 NIV

Doug:

My mother's grandfather was a preacher who made the Oklahoma run.

My father's grandfather, also a preacher, made the run for homesteading land too but settled on the opposite side of the Red Cimarron River. As a result, he had to swim across the river to court my great-grandmother. I've seen that river after a good rain. It's not such an easy swim even when it's not running high. He must have had some pretty strong feelings for that young lady to swim across that river once, never mind on a regular basis. He once said that he spent so much time praying while he was swimming across that river that it brought him close enough to the Lord that he could definitely hear the call to preach when it came.

My father received his own call to the ministry very early in life. When he was only eight years old, he was preaching eloquent sermons to his three sisters as he stood under majestic old oak trees on their property in Oklahoma. He never doubted his calling, and his life of service to God was abundant evidence that he heard God correctly.

As for me, I started running in the opposite direction when I was still a young boy living in Dayton, Ohio. I did not want to preach.

"Please, God. Don't ask me!" I pleaded.

I must have run the wrong way. As a result, I didn't do well in school. I had too much fun trying to be the life of the party. The old saying at the time was "The only thing worse than a teacher's kid is a preacher's kid," and I was a pretty good example of what they were talking about. My grades were so bad in high school that I had to drop out of a college preparatory schedule and begin taking a general course. Some of my friends—the ones my parents didn't know about—were not the best quality either. I began trying to be two different people. I was one Doug Oldham when I was with those few close "friends" of mine, and quite another Doug Oldham when I was around my folks or the people in church.

When Papa was invited to take over the pulpit of a large college church in Indiana, I was thrilled. I told him I felt certain the Lord was in it. I knew it was only a matter of time before my double life in Dayton caught up with me and I would be in big trouble. A three-hundred-mile separation from my old friends would give me a new start. It would provide an opportunity for me to get away from the wrong crowd and become one person again. You see, I really did want to live for God, but it was a struggle all the way.

What I hadn't counted on was that there were just as many mischief makers in Anderson, Indiana, as there had been in Dayton, and the danger of being found out was much greater because Anderson was a smaller community with a much higher ratio of church people.

To maintain my double life, I had to become even sneakier than I had been before. I had to think like both Dougs all the time, to make sure there were plausible reasons for everything I did. It was unbelievable pressure, and I quickly got to the place where I wanted out so badly that I frequently had thoughts of suicide.

But then, as college approached, I figured I'd make one more valiant effort at changing my lifestyle. You might say I was going to give it "the old college try" to straighten up and fly right. I just knew that if I went to a Christian college, I'd be surrounded by people who were living for God, and that would help me get my own life back in order.

But you know, I figured wrong.

I couldn't make it in Dayton where there were about 250,000 people. I couldn't make it in Anderson, where the population was about 65,000. Now, admitted primarily on the basis of my father's reputation, I was in a Christian college of about 900 students and was finding it even more impossible to live with one foot in the kingdom and the other foot set firmly amid the pleasures of the world. I was ill-tempered and there were beginning to be some pretty big cracks in my facade. I fought harder to hold it together and tried to force myself to become something of value.

I was living right out of the seventh chapter of Romans.

I finally decided that the answer lay in getting married. If only I had a sweet Christian wife, then surely I could leave the role playing and the game playing behind and live the way I knew God wanted me to live.

Truthfully, the idea of marriage didn't come to me out of the blue. It was prompted by a beautiful girl who had grown up in the mountains of Colorado. I'm sure by now that you already know her name: Laura Lee Makings.

She would have had me thinking about marriage whether or not I was trying to get my life straightened out, but because I wanted to straighten out my life, I had added impetus to ask her to be my wife.

When I was nineteen years old, my parents promised me they would give me one thousand dollars if I would wait until I was twenty-one before getting married. They knew the statistics, that couples who marry younger have a much higher divorce rate than those who wait until they are more mature. At the time they made that offer to me, it seemed like a pretty sweet deal. After all, there was no one special in my life at the time.

But I was twenty when I met Laura Lee, and she changed my mind in no time at all.

As a matter of fact, the first time I saw her I was riding in a car with my father, and I pointed to her and told him I had just seen the girl I was going to marry. I still remember what she was wearing. She had on bright green slacks and a black sweater, with a perky black and green paisley scarf tied around her neck. She was headed back to work at Mary's Beauty Shoppe a few doors down the street from Tom Dearing's drugstore.

"Dad," I said, pointing as I did, "I'm going to marry that girl."

He just laughed. "I've heard that song before." He knew that every pretty girl I saw was the one I was going to marry. But this girl was different, and I couldn't get her striking beauty out of my mind.

Two weeks later, Laura Lee Makings and I had our first date. We went Christmas caroling together. Soon we were dating regularly.

I was impressed by her beauty, her spirituality, and by the fact that she was so innocent and came from what seemed to me to be such a sheltered background. I bought her her first filet mignon. I introduced her to Chinese food. I took her down to one of the big department stores in town where she admitted to me that she had never been on an escalator before.

She was like an angel who had dropped out of heaven, experiencing so many of the realities of big-city life for the very first time.

Exactly one year from the time I first laid eyes on her, Laura Lee and I were married. Somehow I had managed to hold out until I was twenty-one, just the way my parents had wanted me to, but I never got the one thousand dollars. Instead, my folks used that money to pay for the wedding.

And it was a big one. Hundreds of people filled the sanctuary at Park Place Church where my dad was pastor, and six hundred of them came to the reception. Everything was beauty and love and light on that day, and I was sure when I saw my beautiful bride coming down the aisle toward me that the rest of life would be a fairy-tale existence. I was sure that my days of double-mindedness were over. I was going to live for my wife and for God, and there would only be one Doug Oldham from now on—the godly one.

Such were my plans.

Instead, three months later I stood in the registrar's office as he told me that my grades weren't going to be good enough. My class cuts and troublemaking made it impossible for me to continue. I had ten days to get admitted to another college, get into full-time church work, or go into the service and probably wind up in Korea. At that time the Korean War was raging, and the pages of our daily newspaper were filled with stories detailing the brutality and savagery of the fighting. That was definitely not where I wanted to be.

Four days later we were on our way to North Carolina where I was going to take my first job as minister of music for a church associated with Guilford College in the city of High Point.

It had been dark for hours, and it was foggy as we crossed the Ohio River into Kentucky. I was scared. It was sometime around midnight as we rolled along in a used tan Plymouth Coupe that my father had purchased that morning, pulling behind us a farm trailer that my cousin had built, with everything we owned packed into it—mostly our wedding gifts.

Laura had been working at Mary's Beauty Shoppe the previous day at 1:00 P.M. when word came about the position in High Point. By 2:00 P.M. she had closed out and was home packing. Just twenty-four hours later we had loaded the little trailer and were heading for a town we had never seen that was located hundreds of miles away from everything we had known. Laura had been sick for several days, and the long day of packing and loading hadn't helped. She sat huddled against the door as we wound our way around tortuous mountain roads. We talked about our hopes and dreams, and she took a quick catnap every time she had a chance.

The clock on the dash showed 2:30 A.M., and High Point was still so far away it might as well have been on the moon. A flash of lightning penetrated the fog. In a few minutes there was another, and then another, and then it was all around us, and fear gripped my heart. Laura prayed for our protection and for our open trailer with all our earthly goods. She finished her prayer about the time a dozen huge drops of rain hit the windshield, and I mumbled to myself, "We would have been better off if she'd left it alone."

A sheet of big raindrops hit, and I thought for sure we were done for, but it went on by.

Just then we topped a rise and started down the mountain toward a little town in the valley. The road was straight now and came to a T. The streetlights swinging wildly in the wind went off to the left and the right. As I made the left turn to follow Route 52 south, I saw an overhang and pulled under it just as the skies opened up. As I looked around, I saw that we had pulled into a gas station. The car and the little trailer just fit under the shelter. Not only that, but even though we seemed to be smack-dab in the middle of nowhere, in the wee hours of the morning, and on the edge

of what was shaping up to be a storm of serious proportions, the place was open.

The man who pumped my gas said it was going to be a
"gully washer." He figured correctly that I must be pleased
to have gotten under his shelter just as the rain came down.

The old gentleman ran a convenience store before there
was such a thing—a barrel of saltines, eggs in a basket on the
counter, the big roll of brown paper, an ancient cash regis-
ter, half dozen of most staples: bread, peanut butter, soap.
It all reminded me of the corner store I had known when I
was just a kid.

I said, "I don't reckon you've got a tarp anywhere?"

He grinned and told me he'd ordered one for a guy six
months back but that he'd never come in for it. He figured I
could have it if I wanted it. He couldn't remember the size,
nor could he find the price tag. He said he thought twenty-
five dollars would be fair and threw in fifty feet of clothes-
line to help me put it on. I was delighted to discover that it
fit perfectly.

As we walked out after putting the tarp over my trailer, he
reached over to snap off the lights. Then he bolted the door.

I looked at my watch, saw that it was just after 3:00 A.M.,
and asked him if he always stayed open that late.

"Naw," he shook his head. "We always close at 10:00, but
I had some book work I needed to get done, and I just
thought I'd do it tonight."

I should have known right there that God was going to
take care of us, but I was stubborn and chalked it all up to
coincidence. It took a lot of years for me to learn otherwise.

Running Away

Where can I go from your Spirit?
  Where can I flee from your presence?
If I go up to the heavens, you are there;
  if I make my bed in the depths, you are there.
If I rise on the wings of the dawn,
  if I settle on the far side of the sea,
even there your hand will guide me,
  your right hand will hold me fast.

Psalm 139:7–10 NIV

Laura Lee:

It's hard for me to believe it now, but the truth is that thirty years ago I ran away. I don't believe in it, nor do I recommend it, but nevertheless it is the truth. We had been married ten years, and we were on a very fast downward spiral.

Looking back on it now, it doesn't even seem like it was me who ran away. It must have been somebody else. Someone in a movie I saw. But I know it was me, and I can still re-call something of the agony and despair I felt when I did it.

It didn't take long for the bliss of our wedding day to fade, and for Doug and me to start riding on what seemed to be a never-ending merry-go-round. He couldn't seem to hold on to a job. He kept having girlfriends on the side. He was always promising that things would change, but they never did.

"Honey, forgive me. I'll do better next time," he was al-ways promising. It seemed to me that I forgave and forgave and forgave some more, but I got to the point where I just didn't feel like I could take it anymore.

I ran away as much for our girls as I did for myself. When they were born, he assured me with solemn tears that he would change, but he never did.

He cried tears of repentance when Paula was born.

He did the same when Karen came into the world.

By the time Dee was born, it was getting to be a very old story indeed, and I was growing quite tired of it.

Because of Doug's inability to hold a job, we didn't have the money to provide properly for the kids. I was a nervous wreck, unable to take care of Doug, the kids, or the house. Looking at it now, I can see Doug was on the emotional slide that leads to suicide. In fact, he kept threatening to kill him-self. I was working in a beauty shop and he was working some, though he spent most of his time at home where he was supposed to watch Dee, who was not yet in school. In-stead, he would often send her to the neighbors, sometimes locking her out of the house.

One day as I was leaving for work, he said he was going to take a gun and a Bible, go into the upstairs bedroom, and solve it one way or another before I came home. Can you imagine what kind of haircuts I gave that day? I called a neighbor and made sure she would watch Dee. Doug didn't have the nerve to use the gun, thank God, but he also didn't have the help he needed to find the answer to his troubled state in the Bible.

That desperate incident sealed things for me.

"I can't live like this," I thought, "and these three little girls shouldn't have to live this way either. Somehow, someday we'll find a way out."

Finally, the opportunity came.

Doug was out of town for a few days. I called a friend who got some college girls together, and the first thing we did was clean up the house—spic and span. Then we packed my clothes and the kids' things. Everything else we put into boxes, after which I called a friend who ran a mission for alcoholics and asked if he would ship them for us. I borrowed some money from Robert and Dorothy Nicholson, a college professor and his wife whom I had lived with when I was in college. My friend Helena Sealocks said she'd go with me. She had a young daughter, Cindy, a playmate of my girls. Then we had a problem. We needed a decent car, so we convinced another friend who had a good car to go with us. She took her daughter.

So eight of us were packed into that car—three women and five children—and it was an adventure, believe me.

For one thing, it was the first of January and very cold in Indiana, which is where we were living at the time. We were headed for Denver, where a former pastor and his wife, Bert and Helen James, lived. I knew they would take us in, and I didn't know where else to go.

To be honest, I don't remember a great deal about the trip across country except that January is a terrible time to make such a trip. I remember that at one point we hit a terrible snowstorm—a blizzard. The snow was blowing horizontally, and we were plowing through the drifts. One of the kids got carsick, but the storm was so treacherous we didn't dare stop to clean up the mess. We were afraid we'd get stuck, so we just had to tolerate the messiness and the smell.

Another thing I remember is that we stopped in St. Louis and had some wonderful chili for dinner. Why would that stick in my memory? All I can say is that must have been *some* chili! For the most part, the rest of the trip has been lost to the ages, though I do remember it was a rocky experience and I was completely exhausted by the time we finally made it to Colorado.

When we reached Colorado Springs, things took an up-ward swing. In years past, I had worked for a beauty opera-tor in Michigan whom I really liked. He was a great guy, though not a Christian, and he now lived and owned a shop in Colorado Springs. I called him up and told him what was going on, and he immediately asked me to come over.

He was delighted to see me and said, "This is great! I'll find you a place to live, we'll get your Colorado beauty license, and you can work for me."

I was thrilled! I called my former pastor in Denver and told him that even though I appreciated his offer of help, it looked like I wouldn't be needing it after all. "I'll just stay here in Colorado Springs and work."

His immediate response surprised me.

"No way!" he thundered. "What are you doing in Colorado Springs anyway? Get your friends and your kids back in that car and come to Denver."

His was the first voice of authority I had heard in this en-tire episode, and I knew I'd better obey it. I've thanked the Lord hundreds of times since then for what Rev. James said to me, and for the fact that I made the right decision to obey it. There would have been no reclaiming the marriage if I had stayed in Colorado Springs. Bert James spoke for God when he said, "Get over here where we can help you."

I was running—running from Doug, running from the Christian life that didn't seem to work, even running from God.

But the psalmist knew that it's impossible to run away from God, and I was discovering the same thing. Even though I ran at breakneck speed across the country in a whirling snowstorm, God was there before me, clearing the path and shoveling the snow, so I could find my way again.

"Even there your hand will guide me, your right hand will hold me fast."

I think that part of what I was doing by running to Colorado was that I was going home, back to where I grew up, to the place that held so many happy childhood memories.

I mentioned before that I did not grow up in a Christian family. But it was a good family: warm, loving, and generous.

There were many moments of high adventure when I was a child, living there on a homestead in the middle of the Rocky Mountains. We rounded up wild ponies and used our own corrals for rodeos. We saw coyotes, wolves, deer, and antelope within walking distance of our house. We had barn dances and some terrible snows—all part of frontier-life happenings.

But in the middle of all that excitement and adventure, one of the things I loved most was taking a ride with my Uncle Lew.

Uncle Lew had a big grocery store—actually, it was a one-room log building, but to me it was huge—and a filling station. Every two weeks he drove the seventy miles to Colorado Springs to get supplies for the grocery store. Sometimes Bernice, his daughter, and I got to go along, and we always loved this adventure.

Uncle Lew was a happy, good-natured man who whistled as he drove. He'd get to whistling one tune over and over and over. Finally, exasperated with himself, he'd look at us and say, "Will one of you girls change the tune?" We'd hum or sing a different song, and he'd take off whistling that one until he tired of it, and then he'd request us to "change the tune" again.

This was during the thirties, the depression era, when everyone was struggling to survive. Uncle Lew had neighbors across the road, the Oakleys, who were nice people. They were having a hard time making it and decided to sell out and go to Arkansas in hopes of doing better. Uncle Lew bought their property: the land, the outbuilding, the log home. Before they left, Uncle Lew saw that they were planning an auction to sell personal property, and the advertisement listed a large pile of firewood.

Uncle Lew went to Mr. Oakley and said, "I thought I bought the woodpile with the property."

Mr. Oakley said, "I didn't see it that way."

Uncle Lew just smiled and said, "Well, fine, let me buy it now," which he did.

Within a few days, the Oakleys left, and Uncle Lew rented the property out for the summer months.

By winter, the Oakleys were back, having found that life was no easier in Arkansas. They requested to rent their old place from Uncle Lew, and he agreed. It was winter and very cold, and the Oakleys used the woodpile for heat.

One day my dad, Weaver, said to his brother, "Say, Lew, I thought you bought that woodpile."

Uncle Lew responded with a good-natured laugh. "You know, that's the craziest thing. I bought that woodpile twice and never did get to use it."

Uncle Lew knew that those people needed the firewood, and his kind heart wanted them to have it. I've known other people who started family feuds and carried bitterness for years over things no more important than a woodpile. But not Uncle Lew.

Goodwill—that was Uncle Lew. The Bible says in Proverbs 14:9, "The common bond of godly people is good will" (TLB).

Come to think of it, goodwill is one of the things Jesus came to bring to the world. The angels announced his birth by proclaiming that peace and goodwill from God had been extended to mankind.

Uncle Lew was a man of peace and goodwill.

Those were the types of memories that came flooding back to me when I returned home to Colorado.

How I longed for that peace of God to fill my heart and my life. How desperately I longed to sense God's goodwill at work in my marriage.

Oh, God, I've Lost My Family!

You have rejected us, O God, and burst forth upon us;
you have been angry—now restore us!

Psalm 60:1 NIV

Doug:

For several months I had been driving back and forth to Middletown, Ohio, from our home in Anderson, Indiana. I would go to Middletown on Wednesday night to attend the prayer service and have a choir rehearsal, then return to Middletown on Saturday night and stay until the conclusion of the Sunday night service.

This week had been different. I had gone over on Wednesday night and had stayed right through the week in order to direct the music for a revival. The revival was going well that week with plenty of good music, good preaching, and a number of decisions for Christ.

I also had the pleasure of meeting a man that week who would become a lifelong friend. Joe Moscheo was at the revival to play the piano for a quartet, and today, thirty-two years later, we are still very close friends.

On Friday night of that week, a wonderful choir—The Sweet Chariot Choir—came down from Dayton to take part in the service. Boy, could they sing! I fell in love with them, and we have had two or three very good times since then.

I remember one other time, for example, when I went up to direct them in a concert in Dayton. The last song I had rehearsed with them ended in a big way. I cut them off and turned around to sit down. But when I did, they started up again, going full blast! I didn't know what to do. I looked at the woman who normally conducted the choir, and she just grinned at me. "Sit down, honey," she said. "They'll quit when they're done."

They were so exuberant in their worship, and it was a delight to hear—and see—them perform.

Anyway, it had been quite a week. So many decisions for the Lord had been made. Sunday we had an altar full, both morning and night, so it was nearly 10:00 P.M. by the time I left the church. I didn't get back to Anderson until sometime after midnight.

The lights were on in the house when I pulled up in front. I remember thinking how good it made me feel to know that Laura Lee was waiting up for me. Maybe the girls were up too, just waiting to say hi before heading off to bed.

But when I turned the key and pushed open the door there was no one to greet me. No sound of children squealing in delight or asking if maybe I had brought them anything. Our little poodle, Tangy, was there, but she just stood there looking at me. She didn't wag her tail, or bark, or do anything but sit there quietly, looking up at me with those sad brown eyes.

Normally, I might have been tempted to think that Laura Lee and the girls had gone on to bed, but I knew that wasn't the case. I looked down at our little dog, and I knew immediately that something was wrong.

"Tangy," I said, "they're gone."

And they were.

Laura had taken the children and left me. I didn't know where. I just knew they were gone.

Otherwise, everything was as it should be. All my clothes were hanging in my closet. The house was spotlessly clean— no dirty dishes, not a speck of dirt anywhere. But it was oh, so empty.

I finally found a note taped to the mirror in the bathroom. Laura Lee had written:

Dear Doug,

I have prayed about this for a year. I don't know what else to do. I'm afraid I may be losing my mind. The kids are in trouble in school and I don't know what else to do. So I have left. I am not trying to teach you a lesson. It's just over. I'll never criticize you to the girls. I'll be as kind as I can when I have to explain it to them.

Down at the bottom was her signature, a bit shaky, as if she might have been crying when she signed her name, but very firm.

I've often heard it said that a dying person sees his entire life flash in front of his eyes in a matter of moments. Well, knowing that my wife and children were gone was a form of death to me, and portions of my life came rushing back to me—mostly revealing all the ways I had failed them.

Within a matter of months after we were married, I had to leave college or else I would have been thrown out, and over the next eleven years, I had failed in five different churches as minister of music. Every time we had to move I said, "Honey, I'll do better. This is a new start. Please give me one more chance."

How many times had I said, "I'm going to get it together and start being a better husband and father . . . you'll see"?

Five times? Six? Seven? So many times that somewhere along the line Laura Lee had finally stopped believing me.

It seemed to me that the only really right move I had ever made was to marry Laura Lee. And now she was gone and it was all over.

Because I really didn't know what else to do, I called my folks, who were in California on church business.

I didn't get much encouragement from my dad. "Son," he said, "you have been awfully hard on them. We'll be praying for you."

I hadn't found the peace I thought my father's wisdom would give me. There was nothing he could say or do. I had created the problem, and no one else could solve it.

After I talked to my dad, and even though it was around 1:00 A.M., I picked up the phone and called Cliff Hutcheson, the pastor of Grand Avenue Church in Middletown, Ohio.

"Clifford, I can't come back," I blurted out as soon as he answered the phone. Then I told him that Laura Lee had left me. In those days, in church circles, if your home was broken, your ministry was over. Cliff asked me if I was involved with another woman. Luckily I was able to say that there wasn't anything like that going on—not right then, anyway.

Then he said, "Well, Doug, when I asked you to come over here as our interim music man, I didn't ask you because we couldn't get anybody here to do it. I asked you because I knew you were in trouble and I wanted us to be friends when your life fell apart. Come on over tomorrow. Bring some clothes. Stay for two or three days, and we'll talk about it and see what can be done."

By the time I hung up, even though nothing had changed, I felt much better. It was good to have a friend, and especially a friend who was so close to God, who could perhaps help me find the love of Jesus I needed so desperately.

I was quick to take him up on his offer. Taking Tangy along with me for company, I climbed into my little Volkswagen and headed out into the country. As soon as I got outside the city, I put the accelerator to the floor. As I started into the hills of southern Ohio, I knew that I couldn't go on living. I pushed harder on the pedal as cold, salty tears filled my eyes, and I found myself saying out loud, "Okay, God, if you're up there, I need a reason for living. I don't have to sing. I'll dig ditches. I'll do anything if you'll give me a reason for getting up tomorrow morning. I've got to know that I'm different."

I looked over at Tangy, who was scratching for a foothold on the side window. We were on two wheels, somehow going down the center of the road. My eye caught a glimpse of the speedometer, which showed that we were traveling at more than eighty miles an hour—maximum speed for that little beetle.

I remember thinking, "Well, if we go on over, I'll go home to be with the Lord, and if . . ." Somehow at that moment the wheels hit the ground, the car straightened out, and I thought to myself, "I'll go find Laura Lee and those wonderful little kids of mine."

When I got to the Hutchesons' house the next afternoon, Cliff and his wife had cleaned up what they had always called "the prophet's room." I had been in the prophet's room a couple of times and I knew what was up there. It had a bed, a private bath, but was otherwise pretty sparse. But when I went up this time, I found tables, doilies, lamps, and an easy chair. They had even run a phone line in and brought in a refrigerator filled with food. I'll never forget how loved I felt, and how much I needed to feel that love.

Clifford told me I was welcome to stay there, to go back to Anderson, or do whatever I wanted.

We talked about what his congregation would think when they found out my wife had left me. He said, "Let me take care of that. I will tell you one thing—they'll have to fire me before they get to you. I'm going to stay with you, and God's going to help us win."

That prophet's room was a haven for me. But I never touched the food in the refrigerator. For the next two weeks

I fasted, taking only liquids, and prayed that God would restore my wife and children to me. I was very hungry for the first three days or so, but then my hunger passed. However, on the tenth day, I was suddenly ravenous. I wanted food more than anything else.

But I had promised God a fast of two weeks. I could not break that vow. I felt my life depended on it.

I found myself praying, weeping, asking God to give me strength. A little chorus came to my mind and I started singing it.

Jesus, Jesus, Jesus is His name.
Jesus, Jesus, everyday the same.
Jesus, a name to calm my fears.
Jesus, the name to dry my tears.
Jesus, Savior, King of all Kings.
Jesus, the name my heart sings.

The last day of my fast came on a Friday evening, and although it has been thirty-two years, I still remember what I had to eat. I went to a restaurant where I had a bowl of Campbell's tomato soup and two saltine crackers. It was a feast.

I was to leave that night for a meeting in Evansville, Indiana. I was going to drive all night, and I felt I needed food for energy to make the trip.

Part Two

*A Marriage
Restored*

Top and bottom: Doug and Laura Lee with their three daughters, Paula, Karen, and Dee

Just When I Thought
It Was Over . . .

The old has gone, the new has come!

2 Corinthians 5:17 NIV

Doug:

It had been two and a half weeks since Laura Lee and the girls had left me.

I still didn't know where they were, and I hadn't received one word of encouragement—nothing to make me think that I might be able to win them back. Still, life went on.

In three days, I was scheduled to start the music for an indoor camp meeting in Evansville, Indiana, at the Ferres Avenue Wesleyan Church. To put it mildly, I was in a quandary as to what to do. With my family broken, I was afraid I might not be welcome. I was thinking seriously of calling them and canceling the meeting. And then, of course, I wasn't sure I was in any condition—emotionally or spiritually—to be standing in front of a church full of people, leading them in songs of worship.

My friend Cliff Hutcheson kept telling me I needed to go ahead with the revival. And if I wasn't welcome, well, that was their decision to make, not mine. Cliff said, "You need to go over there, look them in the eye and tell them what happened, and let them decide for themselves what they want to do."

I ended up driving from Middletown, Ohio, to Evansville, Indiana, on a lovely night—if you call rain, heavy clouds, and near icy conditions lovely. But it was a good night to pray and cry—to talk to the Lord. And that's what I did all night long as I drove across southern Ohio, and then through southern Indiana down to Evansville. My constant prayer was for the Lord to bring Laura Lee back to me, to give me one more chance to be a good husband to her and a good father to my three precious girls.

I also spent some time in prayer about the upcoming meeting. Despite my apprehension, I needed the work. I also needed to see if the Lord would bless the music. I had to know that he hadn't walked out on me the night Laura Lee left. I wouldn't have blamed him if he had.

It was about 4:00 A.M. when something wonderful happened. Suddenly, unexpectedly, the most wonderful feeling came over me. I had never felt anything even remotely like it before. My heart was completely at ease, and I remember saying out loud, "They're coming back."

I can't tell you how I knew it, but I did, beyond any shadow of a doubt. God had not only heard my prayers, he had answered them. I didn't know *when* they would come back, but I knew they *would* come back. Tears continued to spill down my face, but they had been transformed in an instant from tears of agony to tears of great joy.

I finally arrived in Evansville around 7:00 A.M. I knew I was supposed to stay at the Carousel Motel, but I didn't know where it was. Then as I came down the main drag from the north into Evansville, there it was on my left—a lovely little stone motel. God had led me right to it. Surely this was another sign that he was with me.

I stopped to have breakfast, figuring I didn't want to call anyone in Evansville before the decent hour of 9 o'clock. By the time I had finished eating, I was really feeling good. The restaurant had been full of good people, talking and laughing with each other, and all the camaraderie had rubbed off on me. By the time I called my hosts, Clyde and Grace Dupin, I was feeling very confident that they would ask me to go ahead with the meeting.

And I was right.

When I told them what was going on in my life, Clyde just said, "You know, I think the Lord has sent you here. We'll do our best to help you heal, and we'll pray for your wife and children."

Again I found myself fighting back tears.

I honestly don't know what I would have done if he had said, "I'm sorry, but in light of all this, we can't possibly use you." I think I would have just got in my car, gone on back home, and never tried again. But thank God, these wonderful people reached out to me with his love.

That was a wonderful week for me, and not just because the revival was a tremendous success, but because those people spent as much time as possible just loving me back to spiritual health. After that week, I was sure God was going to give my family back to me—and it couldn't happen soon enough.

Well, it didn't happen right away.

A month went by . . . and then another . . . and Laura Lee and the girls were still gone. By this time, we had talked. I knew where she was, and I knew she and the girls were doing okay. I also knew she hadn't had a change of heart. It didn't matter how much I pleaded or promised that I was going to change. She had heard it all many times before.

As for me, I knew this time was different, and I was not about to give up. And so, two and a half months after that terrible night when I came home to an empty and lifeless house, I finally convinced Laura Lee to let me come to Colorado for a visit.

She told me that even though she didn't believe I could really change, she would let me come for the sake of the girls.

I was thrilled that she was willing to meet with me, and I began making preparations for the twelve-hundred-mile trip. First of all, I made phone calls to the half dozen people who might worry if I just disappeared. I asked them to pray, not that Laura Lee would come back to me, but that God would have his way in all our lives. I also went to see a lifelong friend of my father's, and he listened patiently to my story. When I finished, he wrote out a check for two hundred and fifty dollars. As he handed it to me, he said it was not a loan to be repaid but his investment in a family that would one day bless many people.

It was late afternoon by the time I headed south out of Anderson in my little Volkswagen and turned west on U.S. 36. I could already feel the knot in my stomach, the feeling brought on by my fear of the unknown. What would I see in Laura Lee's eyes when I arrived? Would my little girls run to me, happy to see their daddy, or would they shrink back, afraid of someone who had already become a stranger to them?

Another rather strange emotion was mixed in with that fear: admiration. I admired Laura Lee for her courage and grit. Ten weeks earlier she had taken three little girls—ages three, six, and nine—and set out on the same twelve-hundred-mile trek with only fifty dollars to her name. I began to wonder what misery and heartache had brought her to the point of such desperation. I wept over the suffering I had put her and the girls through.

The drive on U.S. 36 was tedious, but after hours on the road, I devised some little games to keep myself alert. For example, there were towns every twenty-five to thirty miles. All the way across Kansas and eastern Colorado the object of the game was to average two towns an hour, driving in a direct line from the grain elevators of one town to the grain elevators of the next. The game helped, but not much, and a lot of the way I fought sleep.

I kept the accelerator pushed all the way to the floor as often as I could, but my little '62 bug topped out at just over eighty miles an hour, and that wasn't fast enough when it came to shortening the distance between me and my family.

About one hundred miles into Kansas, snowdrifts started piling up on the side of the road. At first the road was dry and the snow piles from the plows couldn't have been more than two or three feet high—but they got constantly higher as the miles passed. Soon I couldn't see anything out of my windows except the icy walls, and finally eight-to-twelve-foot walls of snow and ice towered above my little car.

Staying awake wasn't a problem now. I hadn't seen a car since long before the last town, and as near as I could judge, it was about five miles to the next one. The reserve gas tank had kicked in just before the last town too, so at most I had a gallon and a half of gasoline left—if that. I wasn't scared, but I was getting very nervous.

The clock on my dashboard registered 2:00 A.M. The man on the radio said the temperature was nine degrees below zero. If I ran out of gas on this lonely stretch of road, there was a good chance I would freeze to death before help came along.

To add to my worries, the engine began to emit a strange noise—a thumping and clattering sound. I didn't know what it was, but I wasn't about to stop to find out. I was afraid I might not get the car started again. Instead, I kept going while I prayed, "Lord, help this little car hold together, and please let there be gas and heat when I get to the next town."

Once again, God heard and answered.

It wasn't long before I saw lights blinking through the frosty darkness. It was a gas station, and it was open.

As I filled the tank, I asked the young attendant if he knew anything about engines, and he assured me that he did. He went around to the back, lifted the engine cover, and began probing around inside. It turned out that the thumping noise had been the pulley belt that ran the cooling system. He didn't have the replacement belt I needed, but he did have one that would work and ought to get me to Denver. Then came the shocking news. The pulley had broken loose and was just barely hanging together. Another mile and it would have separated and flown out into the snow in several directions. I didn't take the news as hard as I might have otherwise. Instead, it was another sign that God was riding with me, that he was looking out for my safety, and that his hand of blessing was with me.

Still, I didn't have any time to spare.

After looking things over a little bit more, the station attendant told me I needed a new flywheel. Volkswagen Denver would be open in another five hours or so, and if all went well, the part I needed would be on the afternoon bus that came through at 4:17 P.M. I told him I was going to Denver to try to convince my wife and children to come back to me and that I had only three days left before I had to be back at work.

He nodded in sympathy as he stood looking at the flywheel from every side.

Finally, he spoke.

"You know, it just might work if we had welding equipment."

"What might work?"

"If we had welding equipment and could get that wheel centered on the flange, it just might hold to get you into the repair place in Denver."

Almost as soon as the words were out of his mouth, his face clouded over and his exuberance faded. It had dawned on him that the nearest person with welding equipment was eighty-seven miles away. I asked if we could call him, but given the fact that it was still quite a while before sunrise, he didn't think it was such a great idea.

As we talked, a truck pulled in and my new friend went out to pump the gas. He evidently knew the man in the truck, and they talked for quite a while. When he came back in, he was grinning like he was the guest of honor at a surprise party.

"He'll do it," he said.

"He'll do . . . ?"

"He had an oil rig that was in danger of collapsing up north of here, so he's been up there welding bracing to the frame. He's dead tired, but considering your wife and kids, he says he'll give it a try. He wants you to understand, though, he can't guarantee it'll get you where you're going."

The man in the truck was the very person the station attendant had been reluctant to call. God had sent him to me!

I had never thanked God for a welder before, but you had best believe I thanked him for this one. Here was a man who had worked all night, but having heard about my need, was still willing to put himself out. I prayed as I watched him centering the two pieces, knowing that if he missed, I might not get to the next town. If he was close, I might get to see Laura and the kids nearly on schedule.

When he was finished, I offered to pay him, but he refused to let me. He said the work he had done for me had helped wake him up, that the weld probably wouldn't hold anyway, and that if it did, and if it helped get a guy and his family back together, he was glad to be a part of it. He thanked me for breaking up a dull night, wished me luck with my family, and waved me on my way.

I sweated out the first hundred miles or so, and then put the pedal to the metal the rest of the way. Just twenty-three hours and fifty minutes after leaving Anderson, I pulled up in front of the house where my wife and girls were staying. I had been shut down less than an hour and came in ten minutes ahead of schedule.

The next day, Volkswagen Denver pulled the flywheel and checked its balance. The service manager told me it was perfect, and that unless I told him to replace it, he recommended putting it back on the car. I did as he suggested, and the makeshift flywheel never gave me another moment's trouble for the next year and a half I owned the car.

Praise God! His "angels" do terrific work!

The Black Widow's Retreat

I will turn their mourning into gladness;
   I will give them comfort and joy instead of sorrow.

Jeremiah 31:13 NIV

Laura Lee:

Walking out on Doug was the hardest thing I had ever had to do. And even though they did it with abundant grace and smiling faces, I'm sure it was just as hard for Bert and Helen James to take us in.

Here I was in their house, with three little girls, no job, no money, and no idea what to do. I was teetering right on the edge of a total emotional breakdown. Bert told me later that he had a great fear that someday he would have to call Doug's father, a renowned preacher, and say, "I just put your daughter-in-law in a mental ward." It never happened, thank God. I don't know what I would have done without the help of these two wonderful people. They were the ones who nurtured and discipled me all the way through high school. Now they listened to my worries and fears and tried their best to help me sort it all out—never judging, always loving, always shining examples of God's everlasting love.

Psychologists say that when you're in a shaky frame of mind, it sometimes helps to go back to the place where you were last happy. That's what I had done by going home to Colorado. To me, the mountains spoke of happiness and safety. So for long spaces of time, I simply stood and looked at the mountains through the Jameses' big picture window. Psalm 121:1–2 says, "I lift up my eyes to the hills—where does my help come from? My help comes from the LORD, the Maker of heaven and earth," (NIV) and I drew a great deal of comfort from those verses during my time in Colorado.

On one occasion, I decided to call Doug's father to ask for advice. It turned out he was in Italy on a trip and it took a while for me to track him down. After hearing the situation, he said, "You should stay with the marriage and carry it as your cross for the Lord's sake." That wasn't what I wanted to hear, so I said, "I don't believe in a cross that is forced on you. Carrying a cross should be voluntary." Then I hung up in a huff. But I did think about what he had said for a long time.

While I was with the James family, little Dee turned four. We had a little birthday party for her and tried to make it as happy as possible, but I knew she was wondering why her daddy wasn't there.

Bert was trying to make my life as normal and comfortable as possible, and one of the ways he did that was to encourage me to sing in church. "Laura Lee," he said, "you've got to sing."

When I protested, he insisted, "You've got to at least try." So I tried.

During a Sunday morning service I made an attempt at "I Must Tell Jesus." It was awful. My voice shook and broke and sometimes didn't come out at all, while the tears rolled down my face. Paula, Karen, and Dee slunk down further and further in their seats until their heads were no longer visible. It was a total nightmare for me, for the girls, and for the entire congregation. Not exactly the healing experience Bert James had envisioned.

Eventually, one family in the church came to me and said, "We have a downstairs apartment that needs cleaning very badly. If you'll clean it up and help Dorothy with the work upstairs, you can move in."

I was thrilled. I cleaned the apartment and the house and discovered that housecleaning can be wonderful therapy. It was about this time that Doug began sending thirty dollars a week for groceries, which meant I could do some shopping and cook for the girls. That may not sound like much, but in the shaky world of a near breakdown, cooking and cleaning provided a heavenly refuge from my troubles.

A lot of people brought me books to read, but the conflict in any story was more than I could stand. The Bible was there, but I never opened it. What good would it do at this stage of unbelief? I did manage to read one book, however, and it had a tremendous impact on me. It was called *The Late Liz* and told the true story of a very worldly, wealthy, totally unchurched woman who found the Lord in a miraculous conversion experience all by herself. She immediately did three things—instinctively. She called an unpretentious preacher who people said could pray. Then she called a bookstore and ordered a Bible and a cookbook. She knew she wanted a godly man of prayer to pray with her and teach her how to pray. She knew she needed to read God's Word. And even though she had never cooked a meal in her life, she now felt inclined to serve others.

That book said to me, "Hold on here, girl, don't throw everything out. Some things are very basic."

That book was such a help to me, and I was thrilled when, many months later, I got to meet the lady, Liz, and was able to thank her for her contribution to my life.

Day after day my inner struggle went on, and meanwhile we were doing our best to settle into our new life. Paula and Karen enrolled in a Denver grade school. Dee and I did our best to make a nest. Two boys lived upstairs and the kids played together after school. I remember we had a huge snowstorm and they all worked hard to make a big snow fort where they played together for hours.

I made a sign and put it above the door to the entrance of our little apartment. It gave some clue to the frame of mind behind the door. The sign read "Black Widow's Retreat."

As much as was possible, given my nature, I was a recluse, hiding from the rest of the world.

But I was about to discover something vitally important: You cannot hang a do not disturb sign on a phone line.

Over the first two-plus months the girls and I were in Colorado, Doug and I engaged in some brief communications consisting of a short phone call or two and a few cards. Contemporary cards with pithy sayings were new, and we sent a few of them, mostly sarcastic ones, back and forth, telling each other off with a joke. I remember, for example, that I sent him one that read "You could be replaced by a computer." Actually those cards were an important step, because as sarcastic and "mean" as they might have been, they were helping us re-establish lines of communication, making it possible for us to at least talk to each other again after weeks of silence.

Then one day Doug called and began pressuring me to let him come to Denver to see us.

"Come on now, Laura Lee. It would give us a chance to talk this over."

As far as I was concerned, there wasn't anything to talk over, but he wouldn't give up.

"I've found the Lord in a real way," he said. "I've changed. Things will be different."

"Doug," I sighed, "I'm just not interested. I didn't know what was wrong in the first place. I certainly didn't realize you weren't saved. I just don't think I can face it."

A few minutes after we hung up from that call, I got another one from Cliff Hutcheson. He talked to me for more than an hour, pleading Doug's case and giving his assurance that he had been with Doug constantly during the time I had been gone. He insisted that this time Doug was telling the truth. Doug was, indeed, a new creation. He now had a sensitive, sincere heart, eager to please the Lord. God was using him in a mighty way.

"Please, Laura Lee," he pleaded, "give the Lord a chance."

When a coldness sets in the human heart, it takes a lot to melt it, but Pastor Hutcheson had been chipping away at the ice that had formed in mine. After hanging up, I immediately walked over to a table on which lay an open Bible. These are the words that jumped off the page. "'Why then,' they asked, 'did Moses command that a man give his wife a certificate of divorce and send her away?' Jesus replied, 'Moses permitted you to divorce your wives because your hearts were hard'" (Matt. 19:7–8 NIV).

Those words stunned and scared me. The Lord seemed to be saying, "This isn't about you and Doug. This is about what kind of person you want to be. You have a choice. You can go ahead and do what you want, but the result will be a hard heart."

Suddenly, I was scared to death of God, so I said to him, "I don't want to be a hard-hearted person the rest of my days." And his Spirit said, "All right then, try it my way." I began to read the Bible to see what it said about marriage and divorce. It didn't take long to realize that God's will was for me to try to put my marriage back together.

Deuteronomy 5:29 says, "Oh, that their hearts would be inclined to fear me and keep all my commands always, so that it might go well with them and their children forever!" (NIV).

The children—yes, the children. How I wanted it to go well for my children. The last thing I wanted was for my hard heart or my disobedience to bring disruption and pain into their lives.

So, after another tentative, traumatic phone call on that line that had a do not disturb sign swinging from it, blowing in the wind of despair, Doug was on his way from Indiana to Denver to visit the Black Widow and the three little spiders in their basement retreat.

Putting It All Back Together

Who has gathered up the wind in the hollow of his
    hands?
Who has wrapped up the waters in his cloak?
    Who has established all the ends of the earth?
What is his name, and the name of his son?
Tell me if you know!

Proverbs 30:4 NIV

Doug:

She said yes!

Laura Lee said she was willing to give our marriage an-other try. My wife and daughters were coming home, and I was walking on air!

It had been a whirlwind day, and the best part of it had been when Laura Lee had decided to give me one more chance. Bert and Helen James had not been at all convinced that she was making the right decision. They thought she should give it more time just to make sure I had really changed and was ready to be the husband and father I'd always promised her I would be.

But when Laura Lee held firm, they began helping with our travel arrangements. Paula and Karen had to be withdrawn from school. We had to find boxes to repack. The car had to be picked up from the repair shop (where I *thought* they were repairing that broken flywheel), and we had to rent a U-Haul trailer (meaning that we also had to connect lights and install a hitch on the car).

By the time we all met for our farewell dinner at 6:00 P.M., the wind that had been gusting all day had picked up in intensity. We were a sight to behold as we finally said our good-byes and pulled out of the parking lot—two adults and three kids in a black VW beetle pulling an eight-foot-long U-Haul trailer. The trailer was actually bigger than the car—in fact the car could have fit inside it. The trailer was not only huge, it was completely loaded down. Add to that the fact that we were driving straight into a fierce wind and you can imagine what a struggle it was to get that little car out of second gear. Only when the highway turned south out of the wind was it possible to get into third gear—and five times during the next three hours I was actually able to get it into fourth.

The trip home was not starting out the way I had hoped. By 10:30 P.M., we were only forty-seven miles out of Denver. I stopped at a little beer joint to call Rev. James and told him I was thinking about heading back to town. To my surprise, he said to find a motel and spend the night and see how things looked in the morning.

In the meantime, he suggested we all pray about the situation. It took another half hour (and seven miles) to find a motel, but we finally did, got in out of the cold wind, and settled down for the night.

I was feeling terrible. It seemed to me that my first major act as a "new" husband and father had been to make a wrong decision. These four lives were in my hands, and I needed to take care of them. I asked the Lord to forgive me for my rash decision about getting back on the road so soon and told him that I really needed him to let me know what to do when morning came. I barely slept that night.

I was sleeping—or trying to—next to the window, and when the first rays of daylight hit my eyes, they were strangely white and bright. A look through the venetian blind confirmed that what I feared was indeed happening. It was snowing. Hard. And the wind was still blowing furiously, whipping the snowflakes along parallel to the ground. It seemed to be snowing sideways.

Fear gripped my heart. I hadn't really had enough money for the motel that night, and if we became snowed in, we were done for.

I woke Laura Lee and told her we had to get on the road as soon as possible. By the time I got back from buying gas, she had the girls dressed and ready, and they were talking excitedly about all the snow. They were excited; I was afraid.

It was difficult to stand up against the force of that wind, but somehow we managed to get everything and everyone into the car and edged slowly out of the motel parking lot. When we got to the highway, we discovered there was only one way to go. Although I hadn't thought much about it before, I now realized the wind had shifted around and was blowing—at a top speed of eighty miles an hour—due east. The Lord was sending us home.

As the wind filled our U-Haul sail, both Laura Lee and I knew that our decision to work at restoring our marriage had been approved by the Lord. We had experienced the first of many miracles that would let us know that God was with us.

We saw trailers turned over, trucks jackknifed, and many cars off to the sides of the road. Somehow, though, we managed to stay straight and steady as the miles flew by.

After a couple of hours on the road, we decided to stop for breakfast at a small roadside cafe. We pulled in behind another car and waited for the people to get out. Unfortunately, they had made the mistake of parking with the wind to their backs. When the driver opened his door, the wind blew it right off the hinges. We saw the door slowly open, the driver's hand on the handle, and in the next instant it had been ripped completely from the car, landing ten or fifteen feet across the parking lot.

We took our cue from that and drove around to the side of the restaurant where we could park in a protected area and angle into the wind instead of away from it.

All through eastern Colorado, through five hundred miles of Kansas, into Missouri, across the Mississippi River and into Illinois, the wind pushed us. The whole first day, with the wind at our backs, we drove seventy-five to eighty miles an hour, even though we were pulling our loaded-down trailer! There were times when I had to keep my foot on the brake just to keep our speed down to eighty.

Our little ten-gallon tank took us three hundred and ninety miles before it went to reserve. We lost the wind somewhere around Effingham, Illinois, and drove the rest of the way home in third gear.

Now we know that God doesn't send destructive, straight-line gales for five people. We can't explain any of this. All we know is that those winds were an incredible encouragement to two frightened people. We thank God that we were there when that big wind blew and that we were able to take advantage of it.

Now, nearly thirty-five years later, I'm sure that somewhere there are people who tell the story of this gigantic U-Haul trailer trying to catch a little black bug at speeds of more than eighty miles an hour—a black bug headed east, out of Denver, on the way to a life of adventure and excitement!

We were also going back to a life without a steady income. I had no regular job. Instead, I was available to lead the singing for various revival services throughout Indiana, Ohio, and Michigan. I counted on word-of-mouth to keep me busy, but there were no guarantees.

When we got home, I had just one meeting scheduled. It opened in a few days, meaning I had to get back out on the road. After that one revival, soon I had another, and another, adding up to thirteen straight weeks of work. Of course, that meant I was on the road almost all the time, which was not a good way to put my family back together.

We didn't even have money for a phone, so every Sunday and Wednesday evening at ten o'clock Laura went to the neighbor's house two doors down the street and I'd call in. We'd catch up on what was happening at home and on the road.

The revival meetings usually brought us somewhere between one hundred and twenty dollars to one hundred and fifty dollars a week, which was pretty decent money back then. If the Lord kept opening doors for me, we'd be all right, even able to pay off some of the huge pile of debt we had accumulated.

Still, there was no guarantee that the revivals would continue. Our only source of income could have dried up at any time. We were learning more and more about the importance of trusting God, but we were always pretty close to the edge financially.

I remember just before Christmas that year I left home with forty dollars in my pocket for one last week of meetings. I was praying that it would be one of those one-hundred-and-fifty-dollar weeks. I was doing the speaking as well as the singing, so I was hopeful. The income from this meeting was earmarked for our food and some small Christmas gifts for Laura and the kids. I also hoped I'd be able to pay the bills until I could find more work—probably in mid-January.

Just as I arrived in the town where I was to hold the revival, my little Volkswagen engine started to skip. At the first sputtering sound, my heart fell right into my shoes. I had heard this same type of noise before, and it had set me back one hundred and sixty dollars. It was after 9:00 P.M. by the time I reached my destination, the house of the pastor with whom I'd be staying. I pulled my car into his driveway and left the motor running, knowing that if I shut it off, it would lock up.

The good news was even though it was so late at night, the Volkswagen repair shop was open twenty-four hours a day. The bad news: It was eighteen miles away in Saginaw, Michigan. Needless to say, I prayed all the way. The service manager figured I'd want it "yesterday" and could hardly believe his ears when I told him he had six days to make the repairs. The revival was due to start the next morning, which was Sunday, and run through Friday night. I wouldn't need the car back until then.

Sunday was a long day. A man from denominational headquarters spoke in the morning. We dedicated the new little church in the afternoon, and then it was time for my sermon.

By this time, I was quite used to singing in front of large groups of people—but speaking was another matter completely. In fact, this was the second sermon of my life, and I was petrified! Somehow, though, I managed to get through it and got a pretty good response, in spite of what I felt to be a rather mediocre effort. Then it was 10:00 P.M.—telephone time.

This was going to be a very hard call to make. For eleven years I had been a failure to Laura and the kids and now it seemed to me that there was more of the same. It wasn't easy to tell my newly returned wife about the car and that I'd probably be lucky to have enough money to get it out of the shop and buy enough gas to get me home. She wasn't angry or upset. Instead, she assured me that we would make it somehow and that our being back together was Christmas enough for her and the kids. She gave me the same assurances again when I called her on Wednesday night.

It snowed every day that week. Every night we had to shovel the snow to get the doors of the church open. But despite the snow and the cold conditions, the crowds grew larger with each service. By Wednesday night, the church was packed. I had discovered almost as soon as the revival started that I was a better singer and storyteller than I was a preacher, so that's what I did.

This little church had a fine organist, Gertrude Leppien. She was an excellent musician, one who could not only play songs, but could also give me sympathetic background music for my illustrations, and as we worked together, God used us to open people's hearts to the move of his Spirit. It was one of the most thrilling weeks of my life—so exciting to see God move in people's lives and to know that, in some small way, I had played a part.

But still, in the back of my mind, the nagging question about my car lingered. I wondered if I would even have enough money to get back home by the time the revival ended on Friday night.

When Friday night came, Fred Leppien met me at the door of the church as I came in. His wife was already at the organ, creating that wonderful mood music that made it so easy to minister. Fred told me he had heard about the car, and he and his wife wanted to take me over to pick it up after the service.

When the pastor came in, I asked him if that would be all right with him. He immediately said yes, and I figured he was probably relieved not to have to make the trip in the terrible weather.

Again that night the little church was jammed. Extra chairs had to be brought in to accommodate the crowd, and we had the largest response of the week when the altar call was given. God was good! After the service, as the last of the congregation left, the pastor thanked me and gave me an envelope with my honorarium in it. Now, I have never opened an honorarium in front of anyone because I don't want the person to see the elated look on my face if it is more than I expected, nor, more importantly, do I want the person to see a look of disappointment if it is less than I anticipated.

But as soon as I got outside, I tore the envelope open and took a quick look at the contents. Inside was a check for one hundred and fifty dollars. I had thirty dollars left from my original "bankroll," so I figured that I'd have at least enough money to pay the repair bill on my car. I silently prayed that there might be a little left to pay some bills when I got back home.

On our way to Saginaw, we drove by Fred's tool company and he told me how the Lord had blessed him in business. When he had been a young man just starting out, God had given him a number of miracles to keep him going. I was encouraged listening to Fred talk, thinking about how very much I could use a miracle of my own right then. I was also thanking the Lord for sending me back to my car with this couple. I figured I might have to borrow money to get my car out of the shop, and if I did, I knew they'd be able to give me a loan. I hoped it wouldn't come to that, but as we drew closer to the repair shop, I found myself rehearsing in my mind how I would tell them I didn't have enough money to pay my repair bill and how I could ask them as graciously and politely as possible for a loan.

It was cold in the car, but in spite of the temperature, I was perspiring.

When we finally got to the repair shop, the mechanic showed me all the parts he had needed to replace and offered to put all the old parts in a box for me if I wanted them. "No thanks," I told him, wondering what I could do with a box full of worn-out Volkswagen parts.

Finally, with the sinking feeling growing greater every minute, I made my way to the cashier's desk to pay the bill. I asked the woman for the bill on the little black Volkswagen from Indiana.

"There isn't one," she said.

"Well, there's got to be," I said. "It's not under warranty."

"Oh, I know," she laughed, pointing at Fred. "There's no bill because he already paid it!"

Nobody had ever done anything like that for me. I didn't know how to say thank-you, so I just shuffled my feet and mumbled something about not knowing what to say.

Fred picked up on my embarrassment and quickly put me at ease.

"Doug," he said, "someday you'll make a lot of money, and when you do, you owe it to Fred Leppien to help somebody else who needs it."

As we shook hands, he put a bill in my hand "to help me get home." I put it in my pocket without looking—following my usual practice. When I stopped for gas at 4:30 A.M. the next day, I remembered that bill and fished it out of my pocket, hoping it might be a ten, which in those days would more than fill my little car with gas.

When I saw that bill, my eyes quickly misted over. I was looking at the first one-hundred-dollar bill I had ever possessed.

As I stared at it, I again heard the voices of Fred and Gertrude Leppien telling me to be sure to tell my wife and three beautiful daughters "Merry Christmas."

The Journey Back to Trust

He who began a good work in you will carry it on to completion, until the day of Christ Jesus.

Philippians 1:6 NIV

Laura Lee:

When Doug and I brought our bungled marriage to the Lord and laid our tattered emotions at his feet, we knew we had a big job ahead of us if we were going to put our marriage back together, and frankly, we wondered if the Lord could help us. We were both thirty years old and had been married for ten years, so it was past time for us to grow up.

I wanted to be able to trust Doug just as I trusted the Lord, but it was not going to be an easy thing to do. Everything we had gone through had left me standing on very shaky ground where trust was concerned. I found a quote that I particularly liked and began working it into a needlepoint sampler: "Rather than money or fame, or love, give me truth." I was not encouraged by the fact that Doug did not particularly like that quote.

All in all, though, I had to admit that things were going much better between us. Things were different now. *Doug* was different.

The Lord had miraculously blown us home with an eighty-mile-an-hour wind. We were back in our house in Anderson, Indiana, and the kids were re-enrolled in school. Doug had already started seeing a Christian counselor at the college, Burt Coody, and we decided that I should go too—on my own. He was a truly kind man working from the standpoint of Christian principles, and he helped me tremendously.

One of the things he told us was that we needed to make a "safe place" to talk—a place where each one of us could have our say without being interrupted by the other. We chose the kitchen table because it was special to us. We had bought it early in our marriage in a junk shop. When we had first seen it, it was a scratched, battered, rather ugly-looking piece of furniture. But underneath we saw the beautiful oak table it had once been. We had worked together to restore that table to its former beauty, and now it became the place where we worked at making our marriage a thing of beauty.

It was not easy learning how to talk. The difficult years had built up within me resentment, anger, and fear, and these feelings erupted in a torrent of accusations. Doug had his own baggage too, and it was not easy for either one of us to obey the don't interrupt rule and to let the other person say whatever was on his or her mind.

We knew we were making real progress one day when I got so angry listening to him that I got up and walked away from the table and into our bedroom. Doug followed me, reminding me none too gently that I *had* to hear him out.

I didn't want to listen, so I picked up a small suitcase and threw it at him. In the old days, such an act might have escalated into an all-out war, but this time, as soon as I threw that suitcase, the thought came to me that I must look pretty silly, and I dissolved into helpless laughter. Doug did the same, and whatever terrible grievances had caused my anger were washed away.

Another time, several months later, I had a sudden extreme attack of anxiety over whether I could really ever trust Doug again. It was a panic that just descended on me for no apparent reason—a sudden surprise attack from the enemy. I went to the bedroom, got down on my knees, and begged the Lord to help me to trust and to get rid of this gnawing fear. A Scripture verse immediately came to mind. I got up, opened a Bible, and found the reference. "Get up and take the baby and his mother back to Israel, for those who were trying to kill the child are dead" (Matt. 2:20 TLB).

The verse refers to the time when Joseph and Mary fled with their baby Jesus into Egypt to escape Herod's wrath. When Herod died, an angel came to Joseph to tell him it was now safe to take the child back home. I knew God was using this verse to tell me the old, untrustworthy Doug was dead. There was a new man in his place—a man I could trust. It was safe for me to take the children and go home, which is what I had done. When the Lord saves a man and changes him, the old one is dead. Now the task for me was to trust the Lord, and Doug, and to give up my doubts and fears.

I had to learn to listen to the words of Ruth Bell Graham: "It's the Lord's work to change lives. It's our job to love."

"Okay, Lord. I believe. I know you've changed Doug's heart, and I will rest in that."

Well, my newfound resolution to trust was about to be put to the test.

It was about 2:00 A.M. on a cold, rainy night. Our girls were asleep upstairs, and although I was in bed, I wasn't sleeping soundly because I was waiting for Doug, who was on his way home from another one of his frequent road trips. I heard his key turn in the lock and the door slowly push open. Groggily, I stumbled out of bed and headed for the living room.

Just before I got there, I stopped still for a moment. Doug was talking to someone.

Then cautiously continuing my approach, I saw that Doug was ushering into our home two unbelievably bedraggled girls—women, on second look. Quite shapely women, in fact, who certainly hadn't dressed to hide that fact.

They were dressed in girlish-looking party dresses—frilly, filmy, froufrou—and both had ballet slippers on their feet. They were drenched. One girl had overly bleached blond hair and the other had rough, uneven skin. They looked tough. Well, let's be frank. They looked like hookers.

I was trying hard to remember that Doug was not the same old guy who had always been a bit too interested in women. I was trying to keep in mind that he was working from a new set of godly motives, but those women didn't look like they were here for a prayer service.

I was about to ask what in the world these two unusual people were doing in my house at this hour of the night—morning, actually—but I seemed to hear the Lord whispering in my ear, "Be nice—or else!"

Before I could say anything, Doug told me what had happened. He had been on his way home in our little black Volkswagen in the middle of a cold downpour, when he saw the two girls standing by the side of the road. They were trying to get some shelter by standing under a tree, but the tree had no leaves. Just as Doug was about to go on past, his headlights caught their feet. When he saw those little, wet slippers he couldn't stand it. He stopped the car, went back, and told them he'd give them a lift.

It turned out they had been at a party when the blond's boyfriend became violent, and she had run for her life. The other girl had gone with her for moral support. They had nothing with them—no suitcases, no purses, nothing. Nor did they have anywhere to go.

We didn't have any extra beds, but we did have a fold-out couch, and I told them they could sleep there. We showed them to the bathroom so they could get cleaned up, and I fixed some hot chocolate. I also rummaged around and found two nightgowns, and then we all settled down for the rest of the night. Maybe "settled down" is the wrong phrase. I stayed awake all night—just in case.

I remember I fixed eggs, bacon, and toast for breakfast. One of the girls covered her eggs with pepper until no egg was visible. Maybe she hated eggs.

After breakfast we went through my closet and found some clothes they could wear—including underwear.

Doug and I both knew our budget didn't allow for any surprises. Nevertheless, we knew these two girls needed help, and the Lord had brought them to us, so it seemed it was up to us to help them.

We asked where they were going, and they said they had decided to try hitchhiking to a relative in some other part of the country. We said, "Hey, we'll help you." We loaded everybody into the Volkswagen, took the girls to the bus station, bought two tickets to safety, and sent them on their way.

That was a crucial experience for me because it helped me believe in Doug's salvation. His motives had been godly. As far as he had seen it, he had not picked up two worldly looking girls but, rather, two of Christ's beloveds who had become lost in the night. His whole attitude toward them was tinged with wonderful, Christlike compassion. It spoke volumes to me about how thoroughly God can change a man's heart and how deep is God's love for us all—even though we are wet, bedraggled, scarred with sin, and scared.

I remembered the words of the psalmist: "But you, O Lord, are a compassionate and gracious God, slow to anger, abounding in love and faithfulness" (Ps. 86:15 NIV).

Part Three

*Our
Growing
Family*

Top: Doug's parents, Dale and Polly Oldham
Bottom: The Oldham family

Star of Hope

Make the most of your chances to tell others the Good News. Be wise in all your contacts with them.

Colossians 4:5 TLB

Laura Lee:

Have you ever known someone who had an absolute passion for telling others about Jesus? That's the way it was for Doug after God put our marriage back together. Doug told everyone he knew—and quite a few people he didn't know—about how he had come to salvation and how the Lord had reclaimed our marriage and our home.

It was amazing how quickly we were able to put the bitterness of the past behind us, and all the credit was due to Jesus. I'm not saying there weren't times of struggle. Certainly there were. But God helped us through them. The girls, bless them, responded to our situation with wisdom beyond their years and believed in God's power to reclaim us all. It was an exciting time, a time of seeing God at work on a daily basis.

Doug started with a small service here and there. Pretty soon we were flooded with calls for him to come to churches to sing and tell the story of Jesus. The altar calls were often what folks in the mountain west used to call "gully washers" because so many people came forward. We made many contacts with people who had problems similar to ours and who saw hope in the way God had rebuilt our home. As a result, our home became sort of a watering hole for the wounded. You might say I ran a nonpaying boarding house for those in trouble. At one point we had our three girls; Doug's favorite cousin, Barbara; my mother; two college girls; and Doug's grandfather all living with us. We were visited daily by people whose marriages were in trouble, by those who were having trouble with alcohol, and often by other evangelists whose lives were falling apart. They were all drawn to us by the hope of our story, and they all became part of our extended family.

By God's grace we were able to help many of them. Sadly, there were some we could not reach. Numerous times God intervened in miraculous fashion, and all we could do was stand back in awe, and give thanks to him for allowing us to be a part of his work.

For example, I remember the time I received a call about a college girl who had disappeared from her dorm. Her parents hadn't heard from her, and they were frantic. After checking around, I managed to find her and get her on the phone.

"Stay where you are," I told her. "I'm coming to get you."

After I brought her home, I knew immediately I was in way over my head. She told me she had been planning to kill herself that day, but my phone call had changed her mind.

She stayed with us for two weeks while I prayed with her, talked with her, and tried to bring her out of her state of confusion and depression. She would seem to be doing better, and then she would be talking about suicide again. Sometimes she would disappear and I'd have to go find her. Once she took an overdose of pills, but I got her to the doctor in time to save her life.

Naturally, I was terrified and I fasted for the entire time she was with us. At the end of that time, I was privileged to see God's hand at work in her life.

We were in the kitchen. She was sitting at the kitchen table, and I was standing with my back to the sink. All of a sudden, and much to my surprise, I heard myself say, "I know what your problem is."

"You do?" she asked.

Even though I really had no idea what I was saying or why, I heard myself answer, "Yes. You're a lesbian."

Now this was a time before homosexuals were so much in the news, and I wasn't even sure I knew what a lesbian was. Nevertheless, I spoke to her with great conviction and authority.

Suddenly, she began to tremble and cry great convulsive sobs. I took her in my arms and held and rocked her. She cried like no person I'd ever heard cry before—or since. It was close to terrifying. It took a while before she could calm down long enough to tell me the hideous story.

Someone she knew, spurred on and empowered by the devil, had taken advantage of her youth and vulnerability. Later, we had an opportunity to open the Bible and see that God considers homosexuality to be a grievous sin. I was also able to show her that the stain of the sin can be washed away through the blood of Jesus.

It was not easy to break the hold that sin had over this young life. We enlisted some godly people to join us in praying for her. After some time, in order to get her away from the other person, we made arrangements for her to stay with a friend in another part of the country. Although it was definitely not quick nor easy, she eventually broke through that awful demonic power and gave the Lord the upper hand in her life. In a ceremony of sacrifice, she gathered up all the cards, notes, and gifts this other person had given her and burned them. And then at long last she was free.

Ever since that time, I have prayed often that God would keep young girls safe from this evil aberration. It is one of the most dangerous weapons in Satan's arsenal, and he often uses it to gain control over a young person's emotions.

During those days, we had so many other people coming and going from our old house that it became something of a joke to some of our friends, including Rich and Linda Sprague. Rich was still a college student when he started a small record company and gave Doug a chance to record. For one of our wedding anniversaries, Rich and Linda gave us a big box of beautifully embossed paper napkins. They were top quality paper—white with dark blue lettering.

When the Lord heals your own heart, then you're able to reach out to others. Our reach now had a name. It was on those napkins: Star of Hope Mission. Tears came to my eyes when I read those words and thought about how close we had come to walking away from each other, and from the mission outreach the Lord had planned for us.

But, Lord, What about My Wife?

> Now to him who is able to do immeasurably more than
> all we ask or imagine, according to his power that is at
> work within us, to him be glory in the church and in Christ
> Jesus throughout all generations, for ever and ever! Amen.
>
> Ephesians 3:20–21 NIV

Doug:

Shortly after Laura Lee had agreed to give our marriage
another try, I was on the road again. She was at home with
the girls.

My father and I were traveling together, and we had just
sat down for Sunday morning breakfast in our host's home
when I was called to the phone because Laura Lee was on
the line. I was pretty nervous as I made my way to the kitchen
to answer it. We still didn't have a phone at our house, which
meant that Laura had to get dressed and walk two doors

down the street to make a call. I figured it must be some kind of emergency for her to do that early on a Sunday morning.

As soon as I heard the worry in her voice, I knew my apprehension was justified. The furnace had quit at 11:00 the previous evening, and the repairman who had responded to her call had told her that in fixing the problem he had discovered another one. Apparently the fire wall contained a hairline crack. The repairman told her there was a serious possibility that gas would leak through the crack into the air chambers and then into the rooms above the furnace, threatening asphyxiation, or even an explosion.

He told her he had re-lit the furnace and that it would probably run for several days or even weeks before a serious problem resulted but that she ought to get it fixed as soon as possible. He advised her to leave all the bedroom windows open about an inch and left, saying he'd stop back on Monday morning to find out if she wanted him to make the necessary repairs.

From the time he had left, about 2:00 in the morning, until 7:30 when she called me, she had been up drinking coffee and sniffing for fumes while the three little girls slept comfortably and safely through the night. Neither one of us knew what to do. We didn't have the money to make a major repair like that, but we couldn't live in unsafe conditions.

When I told my host about our conversation, he just shook his head and laughed. It sounded very much like a scam he told me—a way to get us to spend some money we didn't really need to spend. He gave me the name of a friend in our area and told me to give his name to Laura Lee and have her call him first thing on Monday.

That took care of the immediate problem, but it didn't make me feel much better. Here I was, sitting in a comfortable dining room, eating a big breakfast off good china and sterling silver place settings, while Laura Lee was back home coping with a broken furnace and all the other problems of running the household—and on a very limited budget to boot. I had been gone seven weeks already, and it would be three more before I turned in the direction of home.

Throughout my trip I had had excellent accommodations, good food, the company of wonderful people, and, best of all, the blessing of praying with people who were making life-changing decisions.

Sitting at the table, I began to pray silently, "But, Lord, what about my wife?" I wanted her to be able to share in what I was being given.

The meeting in the city of Drexel was an exciting one from the word go. I made friends who are still friends more than thirty years later. The auditorium was full every night. We were in the homes of church families for lunch and dinner every day.

Friday night was similar to all the other nights except that the people who had invited us to dinner asked us to come early. When we arrived at 4:00, our hostess apologized because her husband hadn't come in yet from a short trip, but she said she expected him any moment. About fifteen minutes later her phone rang. After a brief phone conversation, she asked if anyone wanted to ride along with her to pick up her husband at the airport. It turned out that everybody wanted to go, so we had to take three cars. I remember thinking that her husband was going to get quite a greeting when he came in, and a motor caravan home!

When we got to the airport, I was surprised to discover it was an executive terminal. I had expected him to come in commercially. The man's wife pointed to a Twin Bonanza on final approach, and we started toward the tie-down spot. All of a sudden, several other cars pulled up around us, and we were suddenly surrounded by a group of thirty or so.

We all waited as the plane touched down and taxied to a stop. The door slowly opened. When it did, my eyes filled with tears. There was my beautiful wife and our children. These tenderhearted people had conspired early in the week to bring my family for a visit. They had raised the money for the flight, scheduled the charter, and then set up the dinner party because, as one man said, "It isn't fittin' for a man to be gone from his family so long!"

I don't remember that dinner, and I'm sure I wasn't as involved in the service as I should have been. I kept looking at those miracles sitting in the front row—Laura Lee, Paula, Karen, and Dee. What a night! The excitement was contagious. The people sang, prayed, worshiped. Papa seemed to touch heaven in his sermon and they responded.

Then when the service was over, an announcement was made about a group getting together in the fellowship hall. Our little family shook hands and visited with everybody until the pastor came over and told us we needed to follow him. Nearly one hundred women were gathered in the fellowship hall, all of whom shouted surprise as we walked in.

Drexel is in the heart of mill country, and those women presented Laura with dozens of suits, skirts, sweaters, and hose that came out of those mills. There were over ninety-two gifts in all, all beautifully and lovingly wrapped to bring encouragement to a wife who had been willing to come back home and start again.

As for me, I remembered my silent prayer of six days earlier: "But, Lord, what about my wife?"

God is so good!

Part Four

Traveling Man

Top and middle: Doug, "the traveling man," in concert
Bottom: Doug's tour bus

The Joys and Tribulations of the Crisco Kid

A cheerful heart does good like medicine.

Proverbs 17:22 TLB

Doug:

Life on the road is certainly not easy—for a number of reasons. It's not easy to live out of a suitcase. It's not easy to sleep in a strange bed every night. It's not easy to spend hour after hour behind the wheel of your car, nor to spend countless hours standing in line at airports and car rental counters.

But most of all, it's not easy because it means spending so much time away from the people you love—in my case, my wife and children. Still, I take great delight in all the time I have spent on the road because it was the life the Lord chose for me and the life that he himself modeled during his earthly ministry.

And besides, I learned so much and had so many wonderful experiences during those traveling years.

Some of those experiences had to do with my girth, which, at times, has reached near gargantuan proportions. I feel sorry for people who are overweight—only one overweight person can know what another such person has to put up with. Most of us develop a pretty good sense of humor about it—primarily because we can't run fast enough to catch our detractors, and even if we could catch them, we'd be too short-winded to fight.

I had a friend in high school who called me "Duke." He also called me "Crisco Kid," which meant "fat in the can!" The Crisco Kid nickname is one I've never been able to completely shake, no matter how hard I've tried.

At one point I weighed three hundred and fifty pounds. I had just completed a concert at a Baptist church in Southgate, Michigan, and was shaking hands and talking with people when I noticed a little boy who was about five. He kept staring at me from perhaps ten feet away. I'd see him over there ... then over here ... and back there again, always looking at me, and always with a look of amazement on his face.

Finally, he disappeared for a few moments, and I forgot all about him until I felt a tug on my coattail. I looked down into the little face filled with awe.

"Mister," he asked, "did you really work in the circus?"

I never did figure out who his parents were, but I think his dad put him up to it.

Another time I was in Olympia, Washington, where I accepted an invitation to join some people at their house for dessert after the concert. The wife went home to get things ready while the husband stayed behind, waiting for me to visit with people and sell a few records.

When we got to my host's house, he opened the door for me to enter. There in the entryway looking up at me was a real-life version of Dennis the Menace. He was five, chunky, and his shirt didn't quite cover his belly because his hands were behind his back. His sneakers had seen plenty of battles and the elastic on one sock had completely given out. His chin jutted forward like a drill sergeant as he looked me up and down and then wiped me out with one short sentence: "Golly, you're fat!"

All movement ceased behind me, and the chill of death hung in the room. I was looking for words to ease the situation when a hand appeared from behind a bookcase on the inside wall. It gripped my young truth teller firmly, and then he just suddenly vanished. I heard the pft-pft-pft-pft of the swinging door into the kitchen, a long moment of silence, and then a plaintive wail: "But mom, he *is* fat!"

The little guy glared at me all evening because of the trouble I had gotten him into. I tried hard, but I never did win him over. He'll probably be mad at fat people all his life, which is a real shame because he may well turn out to be one.

Incidents like that one were funny when they happened. There were plenty of another type that weren't anywhere near funny until enough time had gone by. Sometimes it took years. Occasionally things on the road got to the point where I felt like giving up. Other times I wanted the road to go on forever. Occasionally I could go from one of those feelings to the other on successive days.

For a time I traveled with Bill Gaither, and he and I developed a little game we'd play to help make life on the road a little easier. When we arrived at the church where we were going to perform, we went different directions until one of us could get the lay of the land. If one of us determined that we should move on after the concert, we would blame the absent partner. Sometimes the accommodations that were provided left something to be desired, so our game was a way to protect ourselves.

On one particular occasion, the second Tuesday of a fifteen-day tour, it was one of the hottest days of the summer. The church wasn't air-conditioned, nor was the home where Bill and I were to share a double bed. I politely explained that we'd have to go to a motel because Bill needed some time to unwind after a concert and because he also had to make some late night phone calls. The excuses were both true, though they didn't cover the main reason for not sticking around. Bill Gaither and three-hundred-and-fifty-pound Doug Oldham had decided before the trip began that they would never try to sleep in the same bed!

That settled that.

Before the concert, as I was setting up records on my new folding table, Bill and I were hoping the offering would cover the cost of our motel, and the record sales would pay for our food and gas for the day. It didn't look likely. By the time the service started, we had jammed a huge crowd of nineteen people into the auditorium.

Still, the concert went well. Those nineteen folks were an enthusiastic audience. But then, as we went into prayer, there was a crash and a cry of surprise from the vestibule. One of the deacons had stepped up on the display table to change a lightbulb. We lost the table, a few records, and some sheet music.

Afterward, driving toward our motel with our offering of twelve dollars and seventy-one cents, we couldn't help but wonder if perhaps we had misunderstood our calling.

We checked our itinerary and discovered that our next stop was in a town called Elizabethton. Well, we didn't think it could get much worse, so we decided to keep plugging on.

At Elizabethton, Mark Haney, the pastor of the church that had invited us, was on hand to meet us when we arrived. A couple of church members were also there to help us carry in our sound system (both speakers) and our records. They brought us a table for our display, took us to our motel to change, and brought us dinner. Our calling was slowly but surely becoming clear again.

A full fifteen minutes ahead of the 7:30 starting time, the church was full, with people standing two-deep around the walls. When the invitation was given at the end of the concert, people flocked to the altar to pray. Bill played and I sang for nearly forty minutes as people kept coming to pray. After we dismissed the service, people continued to come. At 10:00 there must have been a hundred or more people praying and rejoicing in what the Lord had done that night.

I went to the far end of the altar and knelt down to pray with a woman who had been one of the first to come forward. She had been at the altar for at least an hour. The tears that had streaked her makeup began to flow again as she told me of the letter she had received just that morning from the local school board. Her six-year-old son had a speech impediment that made it nearly impossible for him to be understood. The boys he played with had learned to communicate with him, but it had taken a concerted effort on their part.

The school board's letter informed her that her son, Terry, would have to attend a special school for the handicapped. The boy was out of town right now on a trip with his grandparents, but when he came home she was going to have to tell him that he could not go back to school with his friends. And she also faced the task of trying to convince him that even though he was different he was still of great value and deeply loved by his family.

I thought of my girls and wept with her. We prayed for Terry and for his grandparents. They were angry with the Lord because of Terry's condition. In fact, they said they weren't even sure they believed in a God who would allow such a thing to happen.

I had been back home for only a few days when a telephone call came from Terry's mother. She was excited.

The boy's grandparents had just brought him home, and they had some wonderful news. On the previous Wednesday night, somewhere around 9:30, Terry had been playing by the fireplace, close to his grandparents. His grandmother had been knitting while her husband read the paper when they both thought they heard Terry say a word as clearly as could be. They stopped what they were doing and looked at each other in surprise, and as they did, he said it again. And then another word. And another. It was only a few words at first, but then Terry began to put sentences together and now, for more than a week, he had been talking as plainly as any six-year-old.

You'd better believe that when school opened for the fall, Terry was there with his friends. Not only that, his grandparents found the Lord as a result of Terry's healing. That amazing event occurred more than thirty years ago, and the boy who couldn't make himself understood now pastors a large church in the state of Kansas.

Yes, there were many lessons to be learned out there on the road, and some of them brought tears to my eyes.

Let me take just a moment now to flash back to the first church I told you about, the one where I sang to a near-empty auditorium and the offering wasn't enough to pay for the records that were broken.

I've been asked, "How could you get up and sing to only a handful of people in a near-empty auditorium?" The answer is simple. I'm not singing to the crowd.

I was spoiled early on in my concert work. The crowds during those days were not great in numbers, though the churches where I sang were usually full. Then one Thursday night I took the stage in an auditorium that seated about three hundred people and looked out to see that only forty-six people had come to hear me. I know because I counted them!

Later on I told my dad about it and added at the end of my story, "Papa, I could have stayed home to better advantage."

He grinned in his special way and told me this story.

Sir Edwin Booth was the most celebrated actor in all of England. His younger brother, John Wilkes Booth, was also an actor, and was so intimidated by his older brother's success that he left England and came to America to make his mark on history. The rest of his story we all know.

In England, before a performance the actors all remind each other to "play for the king," much as actors here in

America wish each other good luck by saying, "Break a leg." All his life, Sir Edwin Booth "played to the king," whereas his brother assassinated one of the greatest presidents in our history. The story becomes even stranger when you consider that John Wilkes Booth fell from the theater stage, thus breaking his leg, after shooting President Lincoln. But I'm getting off track here.

On one occasion when Edwin Booth was scheduled to perform in a play, a terrible storm blew in. It snowed for twenty-four hours straight prior to the performance, and the evening of the play, the wind was blowing off the Thames with such fury that the streets of London were virtually impassable.

The cast came in early. They all helped carry wood for the theater's six great fireplaces, four on the main floor and two in the back corners of the balcony. Once that task was completed, the actors dressed in their costumes and applied makeup.

When it was five minutes to curtain, Sir Edwin's understudy looked through the peephole to see how many people had braved the cold, snowy weather, and then he knocked on Mr. Booth's dressing room door to announce that it was time. As they walked to the wings, the young man told the great actor that there were only six people in the theater and that they were all seated in the last row. The young thespian then asked for the opportunity of playing the part that night, just for the experience. After all, he said, such a small crowd was certainly unworthy of the time and energies of a great actor.

Those standing nearby watched as Sir Edwin drew himself up to his full six feet two inches, and then seemed to find yet another inch. He looked directly into the eyes of the eager young actor and said, "We don't play to the crowd, we play to the king!"

With a glance at the stagehand he said, "Pull." The curtain was pulled open and Booth walked out to give one of the finest performances of his life—to an almost completely empty theater.

Shortly before 10:00 the next morning, a knock sounded at Sir Edwin's front door, and he opened it to find a uniformed messenger standing there. The messenger handed an envelope to the actor, turned on his heel and left.

Booth tore open the envelope to find a note which read: "Last evening my wife and I, along with four friends, attended your brilliant performance. We sat enthralled as you lifted the entire cast beyond their finest capabilities. I was honored and humbled as we watched." The note was signed by and bore the seal of—the King of England!

Papa knew I had gotten his meaning, so he just turned and walked away without further comment. His story changed my life. Ever since that time I try not to count the people in the crowd or to ask who is in the audience.

I do my best to be sure I'm singing for the King!

The Miracle
at Seventy Miles an Hour

I was pushed back and about to fall,
   but the LORD helped me.
The LORD is my strength and my song;
   he has become my salvation.

Psalm 118:13–14 NIV

Doug:

One of the great things about life on the road was that it enabled me to become closer to my father. We had never been at odds with each other, really, but I know there were times when he must have keenly felt my failure to live the Christian life, to follow the great example he had set for me. But after God "straightened me out," we traveled as an evangelistic team for a while. I led the music portion of the services, while he did the preaching, and it was good getting to know him adult to adult, learning from the wisdom he had gained through his years of walking with the Lord.

Still, there were some awkward times because we were as different as two people can be. When we would finish our last service in a series of meetings, I'd load up and head for home, driving all night to get back to Laura Lee and the girls in Indiana. Papa would go to bed and sleep for a few hours, then get up before dawn and head for Florida, where he and my mother lived then.

One meeting in Portageville, Missouri, was different. Oh, we'd had huge crowds, and there had been an exceptional altar response. But when it was over on Friday, we were both headed for Florida, and we had only one car to get us there—his. Because of that, we decided to make the trip his way, to sleep and then drive.

He knew I had trouble getting up early, and I knew he would probably wake up sometime before dawn and lie there and stew until the "late" hour of 6:00 A.M. Then he'd wake me up, thinking I had had all the sleep anyone could possibly need. So I told him, "Whenever you get up, go ahead and wake me up too, and I'll be ready to go." Bad idea.

It seemed like the next thing I knew, he was gently shaking my shoulder, wanting to know if I was awake. He said he'd been lying there waiting for me to wake up for half an hour. I stole a sleepy glance at my watch.

It was 3:15!

Somehow I managed to drag myself out of bed and into my clothes. We decided that I'd take the first shift at the wheel and that we'd switch when we got to Memphis, about one hundred and thirty miles away.

My father suggested we stop for gas before getting onto the interstate. I glanced at the gas gauge, saw that we had about an eighth of a tank left, and said no, there wasn't really any reason for that. We'd stop somewhere down the road. It would give us a chance to get out and stretch, and besides, there's a gas station at nearly every exit on an interstate—isn't there?

Well, pretty soon the needle was getting close to the empty mark, so I figured I'd better start looking for a place to stop. The next four exits went by and not a single station in sight. Miles passed, the needle dropped even lower, and still no sign of a filling station.

I knew he'd been watching the gauge for several minutes, and he finally asked if it was time for him to say, "I told you so." I shook my head and told him that wasn't necessary. Then I raised one hand to God. "Lord," I prayed, "you know I've done it again. We need gas."

Dad laughed and asked me if I thought that would do any good. I replied that it couldn't hurt.

Well, we hadn't gone another five miles in that car when the old gal sputtered and died, and I found myself fighting to get the big station wagon off the road. Before I could even bring it to a stop, Dad was out of the car, running down the center line, waving his arms like crazy, trying to flag down what turned out to be a pickup truck. This was the first vehicle we had seen going in either direction that morning.

After safely getting the car on the shoulder of the road, I went back to see what was going on. I got there just in time to hear Dad ask the driver of the truck if he could take us to the next filling station. The man said that he was sorry, but he was only going to the third exit, and it was another sixty-three miles beyond that to the first gas station. He went on to explain that this hundred-mile stretch of interstate had only been open for three weeks.

Then he said, "If you don't mind regular gas in your Pontiac, I've got a tank of tractor fuel in the back of the truck."

Mind? Of course not.

Within ten minutes we had twelve gallons of gas, and were pulling back onto the road as the pickup's taillights disappeared into the darkness.

I decided right there that the Lord had to have a sense of humor. He must have been grinning as he watched his private filling station chasing us down the highway at seventy miles an hour so we could "keep on keeping on."

It reminded me of another miracle I had experienced when God had brought a welder to fix my car—and at just about the same time of the morning. You know something? You can't possibly get up earlier than God!

Still, there were times when the miracles didn't come exactly the way I wanted them to. I think of the time, years later, when I had been singing at Maybe Center on the campus of Oral Roberts University in Tulsa. The loading lights were still on as I made my final trip around our bus to make sure we hadn't left anything behind. The guys were putting the last of the equipment in the bays as I climbed aboard, thankful for the heat that had already been generated by the big diesel. Bryan, my driver, and John, my son-in-law, got on board. Loading lights were turned off. Interior lights were dimmed so they were right for driving and the door closed. Bryan dropped the big bus into reverse but nothing happened. I heard him try the clutch again. And again, nothing. Thus began one of the longest nights of my life.

In eight hours we were slated to be four hundred miles away. I went to the phone to see what I could do about finding alternate transportation. I started with Plan A, the ideal, the airlines. There weren't any flights that would work for us.

Next I tried the car rental companies. But there were no rentals available until 6:00 A.M., which would not give us enough time to make the drive.

Plan C was to try commercial bus lines. We could get to our destination by 3:00 the following afternoon. That didn't help either.

I had a few other ideas, but none of them panned out either. By this time the guys had determined that we had dropped the transmission, so we certainly weren't going anywhere in *that* bus.

While I had been making calls from a phone on one side of the Maybe Center, Bryan was stationed at a phone on the other side, trying to find a mechanic. His luck was no better than mine. There weren't any "Silver Eagle" bus mechanics within two hundred miles.

Our only option was to try to charter a plane. I hated to do that because it was terribly expensive, but it was the only way we could keep our commitment for the concert the following morning. Unfortunately, that too turned out to be a dead end. There simply were no charters to be had.

By this time it was—you guessed it—sometime after 3:00 in the morning. I needed to call the pastor of the church who had scheduled us and tell him we weren't going to make it, but I didn't want to get him out of bed to do it. I figured the bad news could wait until at least 7:00 A.M. Even then I woke him up, and he was a bit like I am that early in the morning. He was up, but he didn't want to be bothered for at least an hour, and he greeted my bad news phone call like a bear who had been disturbed during the middle of his hibernation. And since I had been up all night, I wasn't feeling any more cordial than he was. Needless to say, our conversation wasn't the best.

I didn't blame him for being unhappy. How do you tell your church that the guest of the day is not going to show and is, in fact, sitting four hundred miles away in a broken-down bus? He did have his work cut out for him, but there wasn't anything I could do to help, no matter how much I might have wanted to.

We ended up renting two vans to get our troops back home and left Bryan in Tulsa to deal with the transmission problem. It turned out he had to have the bus towed to Wichita, at something like a dollar and a half a mile. The cost of repairs, plus wrecker service, exceeded seven thousand dollars.

To add insult to injury, three days after we returned home we received a letter from the church we hadn't been able to reach. It included a bill for three hundred dollars—the amount that had been spent to advertise our concert.

We rented two vans to do the scheduled concerts the following weekend, and Bryan finally brought the bus home eleven days after it broke down in Tulsa. In more than thirty-two years on the road, this was one of the three concerts I missed for reasons that were not health related.

No miracle came to bail me out in the middle of the night that time. But that's all right. Sometimes God has something to teach you by giving you a miracle; other times he has something to teach you by *not* giving you a miracle. Either way, as long as his will is being carried out, everything is exactly as it should be, and that's the very best thing for all of us. Over the years I have learned the absolute truth of Romans 8:28: All things *do* work together for good!

Besides, I at least had the satisfaction of knowing that I had done everything within my power to fulfill my commitment. It wasn't my fault the bus broke down. As for the other two concerts I missed—well, that's a different story.

The first of the other two was definitely my fault. My friend Dan Harmon in Johnson City, Tennessee, called and wanted to know when I would arrive for my concert at his church. I thought he was kidding and explained that I was already booked.

He said, "You can't be booked. You gave me this date a year ago."

I didn't know what he was talking about.

"No, I didn't," I said. I was sure of that.

We talked a while longer and hung up without resolving anything.

Three days later I received an envelope from him with nothing in it except a postcard on which I had written, "Dan, this is to confirm our date for such and such an evening. Looking forward to being with you." It was not only my printing on the card but my signature as well, and I knew I had really blown it.

Another evening Laura and I had gone to a prayer meeting at our church. Part of the service that night was a business meeting in which we were voting on whether to install air-conditioning. Needless to say, I voted for it. Just after the votes were counted, I was called out of the service to answer a phone call.

It was Frank Fultz, pastor of a church in Miamisburg, Ohio, a little more than one hundred miles away. His opening line when he heard my voice was, "Where are you?"

Before I could even tell him that he knew good and well where I was, since he had me on the phone, he said, "I have the largest crowd I've ever had in this church, and they're waiting to hear you sing."

Oh, no! I thought the concert in Miamisburg was on Sunday. This was Wednesday.

My schedule had become confused, so I had called the radio station that had been advertising the concert and asked if someone could tell me when it was. The girl who answered the phone told me it was being advertised for Sunday. I called the church to confirm this, but nobody was there except the custodian. He didn't know for sure about the concert but figured it must be on Sunday because "We always have our concerts on Sunday night." I figured that was all the checking I needed to do. Wrong again!

Poor Frank, who had been on vacation all that week, had come home to a packed church, but no singer.

As near as I can tell, the only good that came out of the whole thing was that the air conditioning vote carried by two. Laura Lee and I had cast the two votes needed to cool off our church. I don't know who cooled Frank down.

Some things can never be undone. I have not been asked back by any of the churches where I missed concerts. Nevertheless, Dan Harmon and Frank Fultz have remained lifelong friends, and because they are friends, they've proved their friendship by never again bringing up those times when I let them down.

Anybody Need Some Rain?

He causes his sun to rise on the evil and the good, and
sends rain on the righteous and the unrighteous.

Matthew 5:45 NIV

Doug:

I don't understand my connection with rain, especially
because I don't particularly enjoy a rainy day. Nevertheless,
rain and I have often been traveling companions, and we're
not at all compatible, as the following stories illustrate.

In 1976, leaders of a new Baptist church in Atlanta invited
me to take part in their family reunion service on Easter Sunday. They were looking forward to a big day, and I was excited
about being a part of it. They had rented Tara Stadium to hold
the huge crowds they knew would come in response to the
half-page ads they had placed in the city's major newspapers,
and the hundreds of personal invitations they had sent.

The organizers planned to serve ten thousand chicken
dinners. They knew a lot of people would come to the ser-

vice just to get a free lunch, but in the process they would receive the spiritual food that only the Lord can give.

We all went to bed on Saturday night hoping and praying for a great day to follow.

Five in the morning came awfully early, but I managed to get ready, and the crew and I were on the bus ready to leave for the stadium by 6:30. The skies were overcast as dawn came, and we were afraid those clouds held rain. We hoped the threatening clouds wouldn't amount to much.

We got the equipment set up by 8:00 A.M., and I went back to the bus to change clothes and to get ready for the service, which was due to start in an hour. As I was walking out to the stadium parking lot, I noticed that every entrance had a little pickup truck parked nearby, each with its bed full of ice and drinks—sodas, orange juice, and milk, and that the big trucks full of chicken were already arriving. This day had been very well planned.

I was just about finished changing clothes when I heard the steady drumbeat on the bus roof. I looked out the window to confirm what my ears told me and yes, rain was coming down—not heavy, but in big, splattering drops.

Well, if it didn't get any worse than this, it wouldn't be too bad. Perhaps those clouds would spit out a few drops and then move on.

People were slow coming in, so we didn't get the service started on time. At 9:15, the skies broke loose and it rained hard for about fifteen minutes. Then it let up, and we thought things were going to be fine, so we went out, ready to lead the big crowd in worship.

That "big crowd" consisted of perhaps one hundred and fifty people or so, most of whom were workers, scattered through a stadium that seats thousands. But I reminded myself that I wasn't singing for those people anyway. I was singing for the King, so I went ahead and started the music.

The rain wasn't pouring down like it had been earlier, but it was still falling, and I remember feeling the shock that comes from an electrical cord lying in water on the stage. Still, I kept on going. Then about thirty minutes into the program, it really cut loose. I mean, it *rained*. It came down in a virtual wall of water. And it didn't let up for a full two hours.

By 11:30, when we were supposed to be distributing ten thousand chicken dinners, nobody was there, with the exception of the people who were going to give out those dinners, and they had found shelter underneath the bleachers.

What a great disappointment for those who had planned so carefully, had spent so many hours, had tried to make sure they had covered all the bases. It was all washed away in a matter of hours. There was no way we could even give away ten thousand chicken dinners on that short notice, and even if we could have done that, we would have had to get permission from the government—and you know *that* can't be done quickly.

We wound up adjourning around 2:00 P.M., and those of us who were still waiting around went home with one of the men from the church where we all ate—you guessed it— chicken. Somehow it wasn't as good as it should have been because we were all feeling the loss of the day. The high expectations, the people we thought would find the Lord, the great publicity the church would have received—all of it had been washed away by the morning's downpour.

And yet, the people from that magnificent church did not complain. They accepted the situation as God's will and hoped they would be able to learn something from it. We had prayer and went our separate ways, leaving the whole matter in God's hands, content in the knowledge that all things do work together for the good of those who love him.

On another occasion I was in Portageville, Missouri, for a revival, which the Lord blessed in a great way. The church was packed out every night. The last night of the service every policeman in town was sitting in the front rows of the church. Every one of them had asked members of the sheriff's department to take their places so they could come to the last service of what had been a thrilling week. It was one of those miraculous times when people had found the Lord, marriages had been put together, and so forth. In fact, the church grew in its regular attendance by thirty-five or forty people that week and maintained its growth.

It was one of those weeks when all you can do is stand back in awe and say, "Truly, the Lord was in this place."

And now the following year they were bringing in the big gun—my father.

He would preach, I would do the music, and because the church officers knew their building wouldn't be big enough to accommodate the crowds, they erected a huge tent on the lot next door. It was one of those rare occasions when Laura Lee and the kids were there with us, as was my mother, and I was looking ahead to a tremendous week.

The revival started on a Sunday night with a big crowd, and it got bigger. Every night the attendance increased until finally even the big tent couldn't hold everyone.

The week flew by and it was Friday night, the last night of the revival. Clouds slowly built up all day, and by late afternoon skies were dark and threatening, but it didn't worry us. After all, the tent was new—and it wouldn't leak. We just hoped we could squeeze everyone inside.

The service was due to start at 7:30, and it started raining at 7:00. By 7:15 it was coming down nice and steady. It was really rather enjoyable. The rain made a pleasant sound as it hit the roof, and it was obvious that we were going to get one of the biggest crowds of the entire week, storm clouds notwithstanding. Yes, there were a few places where the rain was leaking through, but we just moved the chairs out of the way and figured that would take care of the problem.

We started the service on schedule, and after about forty-five minutes of music, it was time for Dad to start his sermon. I was singing my last song when the heavens opened up and it poured. Papa got up to preach, but it was coming down so hard that even with a microphone it was impossible to understand what he was saying. After struggling mightily, and unsuccessfully, for a few moments to make himself heard, he finally turned around and looked at me for help.

I jumped up and told everyone that we'd just keep worshiping God in music until the rain stopped. For the next half hour I sang everything I could think of, and some songs that other people suggested. Finally, at 8:45, I knew we were in a very serious situation as far as time was concerned. I also knew Papa had a message he needed to deliver, so I finished the song, bowed my head in prayer and prayed, "Lord, Dad has a message that you have given him for these people. They need to hear it. They need to understand it. And I pray that you will cause the rain to slack off enough that they will be able to understand it."

As soon as the words were out of my mouth, the rain slowed to a gentle drizzle and Papa was able to deliver his sermon—one of the most inspiring, convicting messages I had ever heard him preach.

At 9:15, when he went into his invitation, people began to come from all over the tent to kneel at the old wooden benches that had been placed in front as altars. Then as those people left the altars to go back to their seats, others came to fill the empty spaces they had left.

People were still kneeling in prayer when the rains came again in earnest. I had been praying with someone, and as I got up to move to the next person, I saw a river of water working its way toward the left side of the tent. It came around the organ and trickled down to the end of the altar. As people were going back to their seats, it kept moving across the front of the church, running under those big benches row by row by row. Finally, as the last of the people left the altar, the floodwaters coming in from the left side of the tent were joined by floodwaters rolling in from the right side.

Now one of the reasons we had chosen this particular location was because we were told this lot had never had water standing on it. And now it was standing four or five inches deep throughout the entire tent! We finally had to pull the plug on the organ because water was getting up around the base and we didn't want to risk electrocution.

Some of the men from the church, a few of them bare-footed, and others squishing through the muddy water in their dress shoes, lifted the organ up to the corner of the platform, but still the flood kept rising. Soon the water was six or eight inches deep.

I was standing on the platform when a little boy came sloshing up to me. "Mister," he said, "will you pray for it to stop raining so we can get to our car?"

I did, but it didn't work.

I just don't have much luck with rain.

My longtime friend Bill Hayes told me he had never seen water standing on that lot before, nor has he seen it happen since. God's skies poured out rain, rain, rain, and we had to contend with it. But God's blessing was poured out on the people just as freely as the rain, and we were humbled by the experience.

One more rain story:

I was in Stratton, Colorado, for a concert. Looking around, it was easy to see it had been a long, terribly dry summer. The wheat farmers in the area were having a difficult time. They had seed in the ground, but the rains hadn't come when they were supposed to, and some of the farmers were staring economic disaster in the face.

So, along about the middle of the concert, I felt compelled to ask God to bless those farmers, many of whom had given generously to help build the church here, and to ask him to give them a good harvest. I remember praying specifically that he would send rain to cause the seed that was already in the ground to germinate and grow.

I don't know about you, but sometimes when I pray I'm not sure that I really expect God to answer me, and when he does, I'm often surprised. That's the way it was this time when, as the concert was concluding, I began hearing the staccato sound of rain on the roof.

It wasn't raining very hard—just a light sprinkle really, but it was enough to wet things down a little bit. It continued to sprinkle as we loaded our equipment onto the bus, told our new friends good-bye, and started down the highway. The next night, Saturday, we had a concert scheduled somewhere between Stratton and Denver, and then on Sunday we had morning and evening concerts in Denver.

It was only a couple of miles to the edge of town, and as soon as we passed the city limits marker, the sprinkle turned into a full-fledged rain. It was a nice, gentle rain, but it came down steadily for the next four hours as we drove through the darkness.

About the middle of the night, I dropped off to sleep and didn't wake up until the sun was well up in the sky, about 8:30 A.M. It had stopped raining, but I wondered what was happening back in Stratton.

It wasn't until Sunday evening that I was able to find out. That's when I called a friend, Kenny Scheirman, back in Stratton.

When he picked up the phone I said, "Kenny, did you get enough rain?"

There was a moment of silence on the other end and then he said, "Would you do me a favor?"

"Sure. What's that?"

"Would you please pray for it to quit raining?" he asked. "It's rained so hard that it's washed the seed out of the ground. We've got all kinds of ruts and ravines running through our fields. It has been absolutely pouring ever since you left."

As soon as I got off the phone, I did as he asked. But I never did have the nerve to call back and see how long it took for the rain to stop.

Does anybody need some rain? Maybe you'll want to give me a call. But if you do, it's at your own risk. After all, I don't do well with rain!

Part Five

*God Is There
Even When It Hurts*

Top: Buz, Karen, Nathan, and Jessy
Middle: Doug and grandson Nathan
Bottom: Grandson Nathan

The Mind Goes—
The Spirit Remains

For I am convinced that neither death nor life, neither angels nor demons, neither the present nor the future, nor any powers, neither height nor depth, nor anything else in all creation, will be able to separate us from the love of God that is in Christ Jesus our Lord.

Romans 8:38–39 NIV

Laura Lee:

Life is filled with many joyful experiences—weddings, births, baptisms, graduations, promotions—and God has blessed Doug and me with an abundance of such experiences.

But it is also true that in life there are bound to be many tragedies and losses: sickness and death and disappointments of various kinds. And yes, Doug and I have also had our share of these. But through all of them, we have had the wonderful sustaining presence of God's love.

It's one thing to say from a theoretical standpoint, "I know that whatever happens, God will be there to help me." It's another thing to know from experience that "whatever happens, God will be there to help me."

We've learned the truth of that statement through the loss of our parents, through Doug's heart attack, my lengthy illness, the scandal that rocked us when we were associated with the PTL network, and through all sorts of other disasters and near disasters great and small.

My hope is that it will encourage you to read about some of the things we have been through, that sharing our experiences will make it easier for any one of you who might be going through your own personal storm right now. I guarantee you whatever you're going through right now, God cares, he loves you, and he will see you through!

One of the most difficult things to deal with, and something almost all of us have to handle sooner or later, is the physical and mental deterioration of aging parents. How sad it is to know that someone who has loved and cared for you all your life is getting very close to death, or has deteriorated mentally to the point where he or she is not even certain who you are. That's the way it was for my mother.

My mama, whose name was Grace, had one little girl, me, and she had one little boy, my brother, Glenn. She was a good and precious mother all her days, and those days got to be long because she lived ninety-five years.

Sadly, increased age takes its toll on humans in many ways, including robbing us of sharpness of mind. My mother was no different. On my last trip to visit her in a nursing home in Nebraska, her mind was unreliable. When she was awake, I would talk lovingly to her, tell her who I was, and give her the latest updates regarding what was going on in my life. She would listen as if she were absolutely enthralled. Then she would take a nap, or sleep through the night, and the information she had so carefully absorbed would flee from her mind.

One afternoon following her nap, I systematically gave her all the facts again. With her once luxuriant auburn hair now an unruly gray, bristling out at odd angles from her head, her sweet face with its wrinkles making it look for all the world like a soft-baked cookie, she listened intently, taking in every word I said.

As my story unfolded, I told her, "I am your little girl."

Her face shone with a radiance brought on by love and pleasure. Her eyes sparkled and danced. Her hand sought mine and she said in a voice bursting with excitement, "Oh, you are! Well! I can't wait to tell Laura Lee!"

My mind went to the thirteenth chapter of 1 Corinthians.

"Love never fails . . . where there is knowledge, it will pass away . . . And now these three remain: faith, hope and love. But the greatest of these is love" (1 Cor. 13:8, 13 NIV).

My mama lived a life of great adventure. She was a pioneer, born before the turn of the century, and she had waged a war with the raw elements all her life.

Grace knew a lot about dust and dirt, windstorms, dust storms, thunderstorms, tornados, and deep, chilling snows. Born and raised in southwestern Missouri, she lived in Kansas and Nebraska on several different farms with her parents, sisters, and brother. She worked her way through school and became a schoolteacher. She was a short woman with a soft, little, round body, lots of pretty auburn hair, and greenish-gray eyes. In her younger days she had an easy, infectious laugh, but that laugh became rare as she grew older because life had been so hard. In fact, she became something of a "professional worrier."

She married my daddy, lived in an old stone house, ran a small grocery, did the farm chores, and bore two children. When the dust bowl hit Nebraska in the years of the Great Depression, my parents packed us all up and moved to Colorado to homestead high in the mountains. There they built their own log cabin and tried to coax a living out of rocky soil at an elevation of nine thousand feet—and that was no easy task.

She had great fears, but in spite of them, she would usually put her brave foot forward and step out to meet any challenge that faced her.

Most of all, she was a great mother. She knew how to nurture, love, and care for others. She always kept up with relatives and friends with cards and letters and visits, and she had a spiral notebook where she kept a running account of births, deaths, marriages, and other family events.

Her last years were full of anxiety and worry and forgetfulness, and Glenn and I were finally faced with the difficult, but necessary step of putting her in a nursing home. When she died, Glenn and I asked each other, "Should we even have a funeral service in church?" She had outlived all her contemporaries, and we didn't know if anyone would even show up at the church.

Still, to honor her memory, we scheduled the funeral in her Nebraska hometown, which was one hundred miles from where she had spent the last years of her life. I thought to myself, "Glenn and I are going to look mighty lonely in that church all by ourselves."

Well, the word went out, the day came, and to my astonishment, some eighty friends and family members showed up. One nephew flew in from Oregon for the service, several others drove from the other end of Nebraska, and some came from Colorado. I was shocked and touched by the large turnout, and by the love expressed for my mother by those who came.

We ended up having a big family reunion, with everyone showing pictures of kids, dogs, and houses, and we laughed a great deal about times gone by. What a joy! And a surprise! But why? Why would they come? Her spiral notebook held the answer. She had loved these people, written to them, kept up with their lives. They meant something to her, and so, she meant something to them too. She had made her mark on this world by her genuine love for others.

The cemetery where she was to be buried, and where our dad is buried, is up the slope of a lonely hill, next to a huge field of sunflowers. A road crew was working on the highway that led up to the cemetery when Mama died, so our funeral procession went up a temporary dirt road. I looked at the hearse carrying her up to the hill of sunflowers—and to my dad—and it was throwing up a big plume of Nebraska dust as it went. Then I turned around and looked at the line of cars following us, and saw that they, too, were throwing up that big spray of dust as they wound their way up the hill to the cemetery.

It made me smile and it pleased me. It was so fitting that she should be winding her way to heaven with a huge plume of Nebraska dust in her wake. She won her war with those elements after all. Now she was leaving them behind and going on to glory.

I believe in heaven more since she's there. Why this should be so, I don't know, but it is. And she left behind the Nebraska dust—forever!

I rejoice!

Dust is swallowed up in glory. Death is swallowed up in victory.

Rejoice!

Heart Attack!

There is a time for everything, and a season for every activity under heaven: . . . a time to weep and a time to laugh, a time to mourn and a time to dance.

Ecclesiastes 3:1, 4 NIV

Doug:

The rehearsal the night before had gone wonderfully well. Mike and Rogene Tadlock had a fabulous choir at Central Assembly in Cumberland, Maryland. It was going to be a pleasure working with this group.

As I dressed in my hotel room that evening, I was looking forward to the first of five performances of *Noel, Jesus Is Born.* I looked at my watch as I walked toward the door. There were still two hours and twenty minutes before the curtain went up. That was just what I wanted. I like to be in a building for at least a couple of hours before I sing. It gives me an opportunity to get the feel of the place, to meet people as they are coming in. It's just a good advantage, something that gives me a chance to recoup any losses that may occur later—and experience has taught me that the unexpected and unfortunate *can* happen.

As I prepared to walk through the door, I reached up to flick off the light switch, and as I did, a terrible pain shot through my chest. I crumpled to the floor, where I lay in the darkness. I don't know how long it was before I could move. At three hundred and fifty pounds, I just didn't have the energy to get to my feet. Finally, I got enough energy to crawl around the bed and get into a position where I could reach the phone. I called my friends Ken and Betty Owens to see if they could help me.

Betty answered the phone and said, "Yes, I know a heart specialist. I'll have him call you. Just stay right there and don't do a thing."

It wasn't but two minutes later that the phone rang. The doctor wanted to know how I felt, and then asked me if there was any way I could get myself to the hospital, assuring me that if I couldn't he would send an ambulance right away.

By this time, my strength was returning little by little. By using the bed, I managed to push myself up into a sitting position, and told him that my accompanist, Steve Adams, could drive me to the hospital.

"You'd better come right now," he said. "I'll meet you there."

After hanging up, I called Steve, who came quickly to my room, helped me stagger my way out to the van, and drove me as fast as he could to the hospital. The emergency room staff was waiting for me. The attendants quickly got me into a wheelchair, then onto a gurney, and wheeled me into the cardiac examining room, where I was quickly hooked up to a variety of monitors and other machines. As they were fastening the last of the various clamps and suction cups, the doctor walked into the room and introduced himself.

He looked at all the tapes that were coming out of the machines and said, "Well, I'm happy you got here when you did. Another two hours and I'd probably be signing your death certificate. You're in bad shape."

I just shook my head and said, "Well, whatever shape I'm in, I've got to get out of here. There are two thousand people waiting for me to narrate the Christmas musical."

He laughed in spite of himself at my impertinence. "Didn't you hear me?" he asked. "I said you're in bad shape."

"You don't understand, doctor. I've come four hundred miles to narrate this musical. Isn't there something you can do?"

He shook his head, any sign of a smile completely gone.

"You can leave," he said, "but if you do, you've got to sign a waiver relieving me of all responsibility." He paused a moment and then went on, "Because the next time I see you, I will be signing that death certificate. I mean it."

At just that moment, Mike Tadlock walked into the room. He strode over, looked down at me and said, "I've got a guy in my choir who's going to be thrilled."

I'm sure I had a puzzled look on my face, and he explained, "He's been praying for these last two months of rehearsal that something would happen so that he could do the narration."

"Thanks a lot, guy," I thought.

Mike reached out and put a comforting hand on my shoulder.

"Listen, seriously, I don't want you to worry about it. I always have a backup ready for all solos and narrations. Right now I want you to lie down, pay attention to the doctor, and get well."

He told me the choir had already met for prayer on my behalf.

"We're going to take care of you like you were part of our own family."

I relaxed then. It would be all right.

Over the next few hours, the doctor and nurses did all kinds of wonderful things to me—things that are not a bit of fun, but they had begun, with the Lord's help, to impart healing to my body.

As soon as I could, I called Laura Lee and told her what had happened. There was panic in her voice. When she was a little girl her daddy had suffered a heart attack one Christmas, and although he survived, he had never been the same. Because of that, every year at Christmas she had this terrible, uneasy feeling inside. And now, here it was with Christmas just a few weeks away, and I was calling to tell her I was in the hospital because of a heart attack. It brought back all those bad memories from her childhood, and that made things even worse for her.

I hated the fact that she was so far away and that she was going to spend so much time worrying about me. I think I was almost as worried about her state of mind as she was about my physical health.

Later that evening after the concert, Mike came back to the hospital to assure me everything had gone well and that special prayers had been said for my recuperation. They had also prayed for Laura Lee's insecurities about my health, and they had all been thanking God for the fact that he was trusting them to take care of one of his servants. What a wonderful thing it was to realize, once again, what it means to be part of God's family.

Still, that first night in the hospital was a long one. Doctors kept monitors connected so they would have instant information on how my heart was reacting to the medicine they were giving me.

Thank God, by the time the doctor came in the next morning, he had encouraging news. The fluids were receding and the heart had not been damaged.

It was shortly after noon when I got even better news. I looked up to see Steve Adams standing in the doorway.

He smiled and said, "I've got a surprise for you."

"Good, because I could use one."

He stepped aside and Laura Lee came into the room. Those wonderful people at Central Assembly had wired a ticket to her and brought her to be with me through those hard days in the hospital—and there were going to be nine of them before I was able, finally, to go home.

All through the week flowers came regularly, as did cards, letters, and other assurances of continued concern and prayers on my behalf. I didn't have too many visitors because the pastor had told the people that I needed my rest. But Mike and Rogene came every day, and as soon as I got to feeling better, they brought some board games, and we sat in my hospital room and played and laughed and generally had a great time in spite of our surroundings.

When I was finally released, the Tadlocks and the Owenses took Laura Lee and me out to lunch. During that time they kept telling us how thankful they were that God had seen fit to let them "share this experience" with us. Then they handed me a check for five performances of *Noel, Jesus Is Born*. I protested that I hadn't earned it, but they assured me that yes, I had, and besides, they wanted me to have it.

In addition to that, they had paid for Laura Lee's flight, for Steve Adams's flight back home, for our hotel bills, and for all the food we had ordered. Then they sent us on our way with their love and prayers.

Except for the little detail of the heart attack, it had been a wonderful experience. I left Cumberland with a renewed sense of what the church is and what God intends for it to be. As we drove down the road headed out of town, I found myself thanking God for sending me to Central Assembly in Cumberland, Maryland, to have the problem with my heart.

Laura Lee:

I don't know if you can even begin to imagine how frightened and panicked I was when I got that call from Doug telling me not to worry, but that, well, he'd had a heart attack and was in the hospital. He did his best to make a joke and put a happy face on it, but there was no disguising that this was serious business.

I immediately flashed back to a scene from my childhood, an event that changed my family's life forever.

I was ten or eleven years old, sitting on the floor playing with paper dolls. Suddenly I heard my father gasping for breath. I looked up to see him staggering across the room with a look of sheer terror on his face.

I screamed and ran into the kitchen to get Mama. She came running, but Daddy was terribly sick by this time. She got him to the bedroom, called for Glenn, and that's when my memory goes into a jumble—people running around, me being terribly afraid, and finally an ambulance crew rushing into our house to take Daddy over the mountains to the hospital in Buena Vista. They told us that he probably wouldn't survive the trip, but he did, although he was never well again. He was in the hospital for four months, and when he finally did come home, we moved back to Nebraska because the high altitude of the Rocky Mountains wasn't good for him.

Dad's heart attack came just before Christmas and so, of course, all the family holiday plans were lost in the wake of the trauma. Mom went with Dad to the hospital, and my brother and I stayed with Uncle Lew and Aunt Faye.

When my father was released from the hospital, Mama took a job in a restaurant to help the family get by. Glenn, who was eighteen, went to work on the railroad, and before my thirteenth birthday I got a job in a beauty shop. Daddy was never able to work again, and the family was barely able to eke out a living.

Thus, as far as I knew, the words heart attack meant "your world falls apart," and that's especially awful if it happens at Christmastime.

Life has taught me something about God that some people don't want to hear, but I know it's true. God, in his mercy, allows us to confront our fears. In his kindness, he is trying to teach us to trust him, but that can be painful, and it's not at all obvious when it happens. That's because we're too caught up in what's going on to notice that God is trying to teach us something. Often it's only long after the fact that we're able to see that his hand was guiding and orchestrating it all.

Now, fast forward to 1980. Doug and I had been married twenty-nine years and life was just about as perfect as it gets. We had three daughters in their twenties and a big house. At this point in our lives, Doug had a full traveling schedule. I remember I had just found a man to repair all the old antique clocks we had collected over the years, and I was anxious to tell Doug about it. And then the first phone call came.

It was Doug's pianist, Steven Adams, saying words I never wanted to hear: "Laura Lee, I'm sorry, but we've taken Doug to the hospital. It looks like a heart attack."

"Should I come?"

"I would."

The plans were made, the trip was set up, and off I went, the memories of childhood terror gripping my heart. Another heart attack had come. The world would fall apart.

When I got to Maryland, Mike and Rogene Tadlock, the minister of music at the church that had invited Doug to take part in their Christmas program, and his wife, took me under their comforting wings. They got me settled in the Holiday Inn and took me to the hospital.

Doctors there explained that we were dealing with congestive heart failure, not actual damage to the heart itself, and though it was very dangerous, it was treatable.

The hospital was affiliated with the Catholic Church and had a staff that was warm and friendly, as well as extremely competent. The hospital was also in a very pleasant setting, on a hill, with a clear view of nearby mountains. During the day, Christmas carols played over the hospital PA system, and at some point every evening, the nuns prayed the rosary.

Doug and I looked forward to it. The words of our Lord were there, and it comforted us.

Gracious people from the church came to visit Doug and treated us like family. After a few days of this gentle treatment and pleasant surroundings, I thought, "Where is the fear? Where is the 'heart attack terror' of my youth?" This was like falling out of a second-story window only to land on a soft featherbed. God was allowing me to confront that old fear that had tormented me for so long, and was showing his ability to supply the featherbed to stop my fall. Given time, I knew Doug would be all right. This Christmas would be a good one, the way Christmas is meant to be.

So those old heart attack fears of mine melted like snow when they were brought into the bright light of God's love—the love that shines like the warmest sun, even on the coldest winter day.

Christmas.

What better time to be confronted with his love and care—again?

Lessons in the Dark

Because of the LORD's great love we are not consumed,
    for his compassions never fail.
They are new every morning;
    great is your faithfulness.

Lamentations 3:22–23 NIV

Laura Lee:

When Doug and I are home, I like to get up early, brew myself a cup of tea, and sit in the living room facing the windows. I can watch the morning light gradually bring into focus the trees, the shrubs, the houses that are on our street. The coming of the light is always different—sometimes it's infused with color, sometimes it's just silvery light. God has endless variety in the way he does things. Starting the day this way always reminds me that God's compassions are new every single morning.

Sometimes Doug and I both really need to remember that.

Such was the case on a Thursday morning just before New Year's Eve a few years ago. We had been to a wonderful prayer meeting the night before, had come home and made some plans for a small New Year's Eve party, and then had gone to bed. Nothing unusual had happened. There was no feeling that anything was wrong or strange.

But then Doug woke up on Thursday morning and he couldn't see. The sight in his left eye was totally gone. The right eye was functioning at about 30 percent. To put it mildly, we were shocked! How terrifying to go to bed with everything fine and then to wake up the next day without your sight.

By Friday "the mercy of the morning" had led us to a wonderful specialist who diagnosed diabetic retinopathy with a profound hemorrhage behind the eye. The doctor, whom we had never met before, was a devout Jew who advised us to pray and see what his expertise, the Lord, and the healing power within the human body could do.

Somehow it had never occurred to me to take a class on how to help a blind man, so I was very awkward. I usually walk ahead and Doug follows along behind, but now I had to remember to walk beside him and say, "You'll have to step up here" or "step down here" or "there's a curb coming up."

I was reminded of the way God looks out for us, for as his Word says: "For you have delivered me from death and my feet from stumbling, that I may walk before God in the light of life" (Ps. 56:13 NIV).

I also needed to carry things for Doug because he was unsteady, and I feared he would fall if he tried to carry anything himself.

That reminded me that theologians call the Holy Spirit the Paraclete, which means "the one who walks beside you and carries the load."

It's also true that when you can't see you make mistakes concerning the time of day. Doug sometimes makes tea and brings it into the bedroom for me. Well, not long after the blindness set in we were in Florida for a series of meetings and concerts. One night we went to bed late—well past midnight—and yet we had to get up at 5:00 A.M. In a little while I was awakened by the sound of Doug placing a cup of tea on my night stand. Through my bleary eyes I could see that the digital clock read 3:10. Doug, bless his heart, had awakened two hours early, thought the clock said 5:00 instead of 3:00 and had gone into the kitchen to fix my tea.

So, I sat up in bed like a good girl, drank the tea he had made for me, and then we took a little nap.

David said in Psalm 31:15, "My times are in your hands" (NIV), and it's true. He's in charge of the time we have, and sometimes he will wake his children up in the middle of the night, just to tell them he loves them, which is what Doug did when he woke me up to give me the cup of tea.

Another thing you can't do when you're blind is read. It was up to me to read the Scriptures to Doug. Because he needed to keep uplifting thoughts in his mind, I read some other good books to Doug too to give him something beneficial and helpful to think about.

During the course of our reading together, I remembered that God knew his people would be spiritually blind, so he had all his instructions written down. As Psalm 119:105 says, "Your word is a lamp to my feet and a light for my path" (NIV).

One thing you *certainly* can't do when you're blind is drive.

Now I'm getting right down to the nitty-gritty. Gentlemen, just think about it. You're doomed to sit in the passenger seat while your wife drives!

Now I've been driving for over thirty years—but Doug doesn't know that. Usually, you see, I ride in that passenger seat.

Well, to put it plainly, he was terrified. And what a backseat driver he turned out to be!

I drove too far to the right or too far to the left, I used the brake too much, I used the gas too much. I even used the wrong feet. (I kept my left foot on the brake.)

One day he actually said to me, "Now, Laura Lee, sooner or later you are going to have an accident, so don't feel bad about it when it happens." Oh, boy, did that bolster my confidence!

Still, there was a lesson to be learned from that whole experience: Jesus wants to be the Lord of our lives. He wants to drive us to our destinations. He doesn't want us to do the driving.

Psalm 119:35 says, "Direct me [or drive me] in the path of your commands, for there I find delight" (NIV).

We need to let him drive. He knows where we're going better than we do. He knows how to get there, and what's more, he's aware of every tricky turn in the road and every obstacle that stands in our paths.

One final lesson was brought home to me during Doug's bout with blindness: God's mercies are new every morning (Lam. 3:22–23 NIV). When we were still in Florida, land of the famous 3:00 A.M. tea, Doug was directed by the Lord to a wonderful eye clinic. He had an operation, and the sight in his eye gradually came back. It was like sitting in our front room in the morning darkness and watching as God gradually turns on the light of the new day and things slowly come into sharper focus. Sometimes the darkness in our lives can be very real, but if we will give it to him, knowing that he always knows best and gives what is best, God can make something beautiful out of the darkest days we've ever experienced.

Of course, I was delighted that Doug's blindness was only temporary and that God brought us through it. But if the blindness hadn't happened, I never would have learned in such a deeper way that God knew we would be spiritually blind, and therefore, gave himself

to direct our paths,

to carry our loads,

to wake us in the night with his love,

to instruct us in his word,

to drive us to our destinations,

to remind us that his mercies are new every morning.

Yes, thanks to God, there is hope! There is hope in times of marital difficulty. There is hope when unpleasant changes and illness come into a life. There is hope when we lose loved ones to death or are facing death ourselves. There is *always* hope in God's unfathomable, never-failing, life-giving love!

God Knows Where You Are

My soul finds rest in God alone;
  my salvation comes from him.
He alone is my rock and my salvation;
  he is my fortress, I will never be shaken.

Psalm 62:1–2 NIV

Laura Lee:

Illness never comes on slowly with me. Instead, it comes in a huge hurry, rushing in, knocking my feet out from under me, and suddenly I'm an emergency case and I'm so close to death I can feel death's icy fingers brushing against my cheek.

That's the way it had happened before, and that's the way it happened again.

After three hours of delicate surgery to correct a blockage in my small intestine, followed by six days in intensive care, I was finally taken into a regular room. Room 229 to be exact. I was glad to be there, thrilled to be alive.

The girls, bless their hearts, were taking turns caring for me and Doug. He was recovering from his eye surgery after having been blind for nearly three months. Dee had made a long run from Nashville to take care of us for the first few days after my surgery. Karen was to follow that up by coming from her home in New Jersey for four or five days, and then Paula, who lives in town, would take care of the time that was left.

On the day Karen was due to come, she taught all day at her school, went home and got things organized so her family would fare okay during her absence, and then started out of her driveway in the dark all alone. She stopped at the end of the driveway and breathed a quick prayer: "Lord, I'm afraid to do this alone at night. Maybe I'm not smart enough to do it. Please put angels all around me."

She also stopped at a convenience store and bought herself a hot cup of broccoli soup. That soup didn't sit too well. By the time she got onto the New Jersey Turnpike she was feeling very sick. And to make things even worse, a terrible storm had come up. The wind was rocking the car, and the rain was coming down so fast that her windshield wipers seemed to be useless in the face of it.

When she finally found a rest area along the turnpike, she was feeling deathly ill and wondering if she could even go on. She stopped and got out, fighting wind so hard that she didn't dare to put up her umbrella for fear the wind would rip it right out of her hand. She was drenched by the time she got to the ladies' room, where she said good-bye to the soup. After hanging around for a while, she finally felt better and decided she could continue the trip.

The storm didn't get better though—it increased and turned to sleet as she reached the beltway in Washington, D.C. After a two-hour traffic ordeal there, she knew she was too tired to go on and would have to stop for the night.

She saw a sign that said "Manassas, Business Route" and thought, "Great! Motels!" She was wrong. This road went through the Manassas Battlefield area on its way to Manassas. She was on a two-lane, hilly road in an awful storm, following the only other car on the road.

After miles and miles of this, she came to a busy intersection, and through the darkness and the storm, she was able to make out some motel signs blinking in the distance. She found a pay phone—one that hadn't had the phone book ripped out of it—and started calling motels in the area. Her luck wasn't about to change. They were all full.

Fighting back tears, she decided she had no choice but to keep moving in our direction. She went back to her car, started the engine, and headed back down the highway. She hadn't gone too far when she saw the flash of another motel sign a quarter of a mile or so ahead of her.

Her first impulse was to go on. She'd made enough calls to know that nobody in this area had any vacancies. But then, as she was about to drive on past, she thought, "One more try," and impulsively pulled into their parking lot.

She fought her way in through the rain and sleet and asked the clerk who greeted her, "You wouldn't by any chance have a room, would you?"

"Well, you know all the motels have filled up because of the storm."

"Yes, I know." She turned around to leave.

"Oh . . . but . . . wait a minute. Looks like you're in luck. We've just had a cancellation. Do you want it?"

What a silly question! Of course she wanted it. She signed the form and he handed her the key . . . room 229.

Tears filled her eyes when she saw that room key. I was in room 229 in the hospital. She would be in room 229 in a motel. She told me later it was like God was saying to her, "I know where you are, and I know where your mother is, and I'm watching over both of you."

She knew then that everything was under control. She thanked the clerk, went to her room, thanked the Lord for putting his angels all around her, and had a peaceful night's sleep. It was around noon when she walked into room 229 in the hospital, where we both thanked the Lord for his constant loving care.

Yes, God is good, and Karen had come safely through the storm.

If you're sick or alone in a dark place or in an awful storm in your life, never fear. God knows where you are!

I had learned this lesson on another occasion a few years earlier when I had wound up staying in the hospital for more than a month, spending most of that time in intensive care. The three girls and Doug were taking turns staying with me, day and night, and even though they loved me very much, they were tired and their endurance was wearing thin.

It was especially difficult for them because I often had hallucinations that threw me into panic and fear. If they were in the room, it was easier for me to get reoriented, but it was difficult for them to listen to me talk out of my mind or to see me cower in fear from unseen enemies.

Finally, when I was showing signs of improvement, they decided that surely the nurses could handle the night shift, so they worked out a plan. Doug was to come in at supper time and stay until almost bedtime when he would be relieved by Karen and Paula, who would both come in, visit a while, reassure me, and then go home to a real bed for the night.

The plan worked great. Then one night Doug left and both of the girls came in, one standing on either side of the bed. They started to tell me they were both going home when I looked up at them and said, "Janie DeSaegher's couch is upside down in my mouth. Will you get it out?" Paula and Karen looked at each other and each of them whispered, "I'll stay."

I don't know which of them stayed. Perhaps both did.

We laughed about that "upside down couch" in my mouth when I was finally well enough to go home. I have no idea what I was thinking, but I'm sure that at the time I just desperately wanted that old couch out of my mouth.

When I think about how my family took care of me during those dark days, it still brings tears to my eyes. I've never heard a better example of the love of a family. But you know, it is the same spirit of love that indwells the family of God—the church. Whereas other people would walk out on you, a Christian brother or sister will go the extra mile, stay the night, put themselves out—whatever it takes to see you through your time of trouble.

There is a reason for this. The true Christian does these hard things as if he were doing them for the Lord, remembering the saying of Jesus recorded in Matthew 25:37–40: "Then the righteous will answer him, 'Lord, when did we see you hungry and feed you, or thirsty and give you something to drink? When did we see you a stranger and invite you in, or needing clothes and clothe you? When did we see you sick or in prison and go to visit you?'

"The King will reply, 'I tell you the truth, whatever you did for one of the least of these brothers of mine, you did for me'" (NIV).

That's the reason Paula or Karen or perhaps both of them sat up one more night in a hard, uncomfortable hospital chair. Not only because I was their mother, but because they were doing it as unto the Lord.

And surely the Lord was with me during that difficult time in the hospital. His love even came to me in the form of an old English sheepdog. Let me explain.

As I mentioned earlier, while I was in the hospital, I frequently suffered from hallucinations—that "couch" in my mouth being a good example. In my confused mental state, I visited with friends who weren't really there and asked the nurses to quiet down children who were playing around the desk, when there were no children at all. No wonder we're commanded to pray for each other. There certainly isn't any way to pray for yourself when your mind is out of whack the way mine was.

Well, one day I "saw" an old English sheepdog going from door to door at the hospital, trying to get in. I knew if that dog could just get to my room, he would comfort me. I knew that beyond any doubt. Oh, how I wanted to put my arms around that dog and pet his shaggy head.

Doug came in about that time and I said, "Let him in."

He looked around to see who I was talking about and then asked, "Let who in?"

"The old English sheepdog," I said, with just a hint of impatience.

"*What* old English sheepdog?"

"The one that's trying to get in so he can come and comfort me! Let him in!"

Doug put his hand on my shoulder to reassure me. "Laura Lee, there is no dog."

"Yes, there is," I insisted.

"No there isn't. Now calm down."

I dissolved into tears wondering how Doug could be so mean, and he sat there in a miserable heap, a poor soul with a crazy woman for a wife.

I admit that would be kind of sad if it were the end of the story, but it's not.

Fast forward about three years, after God restored my health through the wonder of a surgery called an ileostomy.

Doug had spent most of twenty-five years on the road doing concerts, but for the last six or seven he had done very few. And then a new booking agency came to us and offered to start scheduling Doug into some churches again.

We decided to give it a try, with the stipulation that I'd travel with him. It would be an adventure where we could enjoy traveling together, as well as give honor and glory to God through the concerts.

For about six months we gave it everything we had, and we were enjoying the experience. We had fun traveling together, met some fabulous church people, and gave some good concerts. But something was happening that we never expected. We were losing money. Somehow we were spending more than we were making.

So we sat down and had a time of "Let's think this thing through." We did a lot of talking, made some changes in booking, prayed a lot, and seriously asked for God's guidance.

About this time I prayed a foolish prayer, a prayer that nobody knew anything about except me and God.

My prayer went something like this: "Dear Lord, you know we're confused about what to do. Should we continue to do concerts or hang it up? Let's see, how will we know? Here's a fleece—if we're supposed to keep doing concerts, have someone give us an old English sheepdog, or let us find one that's cheap enough for us to afford." (Those dogs cost several hundred dollars, and we didn't have that kind of money to spend.)

I think what I was still secretly trying to do was to get that dog through the door of my hospital room to comfort me. I don't give up easy, you see.

A couple of months later, Doug and I were on the road somewhere and talking to Dee on the phone.

She said, "Mom, remember those people on the other side of town who breed old English sheepdogs?"

"Yes?"

"Well, they just called me. The lady said Vernon Brewer (a friend of ours) had bought one of their puppies, but because someone in his family was allergic to it, he had to bring it back."

"Oh, that's too bad," I said, not yet understanding what she was getting at.

"Well, Mr. Brewer put two hundred dollars down on it, so all she wants now is two hundred dollars. Can I go look at it?"

I said, "Dee, we're gone a lot. It would be your dog. You'd have to train it and everything. Please, think this through carefully."

"Okay, Mom. We'll see."

A couple of days later we called back home and asked her what she did about the dog.

"Her name is Gracie," Dee said, "and she likes it here very much."

Now that Gracie was signed, sealed, and delivered, I told Dee and Doug about my prayer, much to their amazement.

Don't you think that when a dog becomes your answer to a prayer for guidance, it means that she is a "spiritual dog"? That's why I have a special name for the dog. Everyone else may think her name is Gracie, but I call her Amazing Grace.

Every time I look at that dog, I'm reminded that even in the most difficult times of life, God is there, reaching out to us, expressing his loving care in as many ways as he can.

I learned a similar lesson a few weeks after I got home from the hospital. As you can imagine, a lot of things had piled up and had gone untended to while I was sick.

Once I was better, I decided to go out and check on some things we had in storage. We had a lot of stuff we didn't have room for at home, so we had stored it in the cheapest place available, which happened to be out in the country—a converted farm building that was painted a flat, depressing black.

I went there by myself, ten miles out in the country, where the building sat on top of a windy hill. It was a little spooky to be sure.

I wrestled the lock open and immediately was almost overcome by the damp, nauseating smell of mildew. As I entered the storage area, the reason for the smell immediately became obvious. The roof had been leaking for goodness knows how long. Boxes and boxes of our things had become soaked and now reeked of mildew.

Over in the corner, under the very worst leak of all, sat two big metal files, files full of my father-in-law's sermons—some of our most cherished possessions. Doug's father had long since gone home to be with God, but he had left behind dozens of his sermons, all of which had been written out and delivered almost word for word from the pulpit. He was such a dynamic speaker that no one ever suspected he was reading. And as for the sermons themselves, they were so perfectly written that they could have been published in book form, virtually without editing. They had been filed away in perfect order.

I pulled the drawers open in fear and trembling. My fears were justified. All of the sermons were wet. The ones on the bottom shelves were soaked through, while those on the higher shelves were wet and stuck together.

I was overcome with two distinct emotions—anger and panic. My anger was directed at the man who had rented us this place. He should have made sure that our things were protected from the elements. In an ill-tempered frenzy I began to pull those sermons out of the drawers and take them outside, messing the order up in the process. I spread them out—some on the car and others on the ground, putting rocks on them as I did to keep them from blowing away.

I was so sick about it that angry, frustrated tears were rolling down my face. On and on I worked, crying harder and getting madder by the minute.

I was having what we used to call a "tizzy-fit." It was such an impossible tragedy, and I wondered how I would ever tell Doug that all of his father's precious sermons were ruined. He would be devastated.

At the height of my tizzy-fit, I grabbed one of the sermons, preparing to put it on the ground and put a rock on top of it. As I turned it over, the words leaped out at me: "Be thankful in all things."

I was so surprised that I said out loud, "What did you say?"

I read it again. "Be thankful in all things." It was as if Doug's father were there speaking to me personally, telling me I needed to calm down, to be thankful in spite of this mess.

It seemed as if Dale Oldham had briefly stepped out of heaven and had come to that windy hillside strewn with his sermons, had taken me gently by the shoulders, given me a little shake and a grin and said, "Straighten up. Be thankful in *all* things."

So that's what I did. It took all my emotional energy, but I straightened up. And as it turned out, I was able to save most of the sermons. And while I was doing it, I was thanking the Lord for his many blessings in my life, not the least of which was Doug's father—a godly man, someone to follow.

I was also thinking of 1 Thessalonians 2:11–12: "For you know that we dealt with each of you as a father deals with his own children, encouraging, comforting and urging you to live lives worthy of God, who calls you into his kingdom and glory" (NIV).

Thank you, Papa!

High and Lifted Up

Arise, shine, for your light has come,
and the glory of the LORD rises upon you.

Isaiah 60:1 NIV

Laura Lee:

How my heart breaks for those who don't know that, thanks to the incredible love of Jesus, life on this planet is only a prelude to the glory that is yet to come.

It was Christmas.

We pulled our mini-bus up on the little hill at the side of the house. There were a dozen or so of us, and we piled out, talking and laughing. We were caroling and had come out to the lake to sing for Jennifer and Robin.

We had to walk down the hill a few steps to the house from the bus or else go down the driveway, which led to the carport and the back door. Their house sits right up against and over the lake, so there is no front door.

Someone knocked on the back door, and when Jennifer and Robin, followed by their two teenage daughters, opened it, we all burst into song. But in the middle of the song, I had to stop singing and just drink in the scene. It looked like a Currier and Ives print. Some of the singers were on the steps of the driveway while others stood near the door, and it looked for all the world as if a set director had spent hours making sure everybody knew exactly where to stand. It looked perfect.

Jennifer and Robin stood in the doorway, their arms wrapped around each other, the two girls standing behind them, the lights from the carport and the open door making it look as if a spotlight were shining on them.

We were ending our little concert with "We Wish You a Merry Christmas," when I realized that all the singers had tears in their eyes or tears slowly trickling down their cheeks—including me.

We all knew that Jennifer had cancer, that this might be her last Christmas on this earth. That's why, when the girls brought out some cookies they had baked, I had a very hard time getting mine to go down over the lump in my throat.

"She's too young to die," I thought. "She's too wonderful to die. Robin needs her. The girls need her. We all need her. Jennifer is, well, Jennifer."

She came into my life nearly four years ago, when I was trying to recover from an illness that almost took my life—ulcerative colitis. When I finally came home after thirty-eight days in the hospital, I couldn't walk, couldn't write, had lost my hair, and had to have help on a daily basis to take care of myself.

When we asked the ladies' group at church to announce that we needed someone to help me when Doug and the girls were too busy, Jennifer volunteered. Not that she needed anything to do. She already helped run a youth camp, did church work, prepared taxes for people, and had her husband and children to take care of. But despite all that, she came anyway, trailing sunshine and chasing shadows away. She told me funny stories, brought interesting videos, and shared her heart with me as she went about her nursing duties.

Jennifer had platinum blond hair that didn't come out of a bottle, gorgeous, clear alabaster skin, and a smile that could light up the darkest room. I loved her, and she helped me want to get up and live again. She was absolutely wonderful to me.

A year or so after that, we were looking for someone to teach our grandson, John, to ride horses. We found out that in addition to her many other talents, Jennifer was an excellent horsewoman who sometimes gave riding lessons. So John and his friend Jarod began taking lessons from her. She always told me, "I've never in my life seen such courteous little boys. Even when they're just talking to each other, I hear them saying polite things. It blows me away." She was always so quick to share an encouraging word or a happy thought.

Then one fall, just before Thanksgiving, Jennifer was diagnosed with breast cancer and went into the hospital for surgery. We were all stunned because Jennifer was too much alive to ever be sick.

She was still in the hospital on Thanksgiving, so we invited Robin and the girls to our house for dinner, and then we loaded up a plate and took it to Jennifer.

Doug and I went to a prayer meeting on Sunday evening and I prayed mightily for her—giving the Lord some terrific arguments for healing her that were perilously close to ultimatums. And then suddenly, as if in answer to my prayers, in my mind's eye I saw her—as in a vision—and she was glowing. She was lifted up from the earth, with her beautiful, pale hair shining, a radiant smile on her lips, and she seemed to be more real and alive than any earthly person could ever be.

The image faded as quickly as it had come, and I asked the Lord, "What does this mean? Is she healed? Or does it mean she's going to rise above us all?" There was no discernible answer.

Well, the radical surgery went well and she was every doctor's dream of a good patient. She recovered, picked up her duties, and everyone sighed a big sigh as life returned to normal.

When summer came, she got pneumonia and had to be hospitalized. She got out in time to help Robin with a wilderness camping trip. Then she started experiencing trouble with her lungs again. This time it wasn't pneumonia, but cancer.

First it was in the lungs, then the bones in the leg, then the skull, followed by the liver. It was spreading fast.

Despite it all, her attitude was tremendous. She was helping everyone else deal with her cancer instead of the other way around. She even came to church, gave a testimony, and sang "My Redeemer Is Faithful and True." She told me she was happy for every day the Lord gave her, and added that she and Robin had already made funeral arrangements.

"You know, Laura Lee," she told me, "I'm so claustrophobic. The only thing that's hard for me is thinking about the coffin. I can't stand to be in a closed-up box."

I was able to say, with more certainty than I've ever said anything, "Jennifer, *you* will not be in that box. I *saw* you, high and lifted up, transcendent, glowing, and more *you* than you've ever been, but somehow, not subject to the decay of this world. I *saw* you! That's where *you* will be—on your way to glory, in a glorified body! You will be high and lifted up, and shining."

On October 20 she was, indeed, high and lifted up. I know she is shining now, and she will shine forever!

Doug:

Why didn't God choose to heal Jennifer, instead of taking her home to be with him? I wish I knew, but I don't. God has his purposes, and I know they are best, and I rest in that. Otherwise, healing is something I'll probably never understand. I know God heals, but I don't know how or why or when he decides to heal—to interrupt the natural order of things with a supernatural act.

I remember one time when I was in Greenville, North Carolina, for a concert. After the concert was over, the crowd was slow to leave. As I usually did at my concerts, I stayed down front to talk to the people who had questions or comments. Finally, when the building was nearly empty, I watched an elderly couple coming down the aisle toward me.

They were happy and laughing together as they came, but I noticed that she walked slightly behind him, holding his arm. I was certain she was blind, and I was afraid they were coming for prayer.

I was relieved, when they finally got to me, by their good-natured conversation. They told me all about their children, how old they were when they had made their decisions for Christ—all sorts of things. As they talked, the love they felt for the Lord and for each other just bubbled out of them. Maybe they weren't going to ask for prayer after all.

But then the man's face clouded over. Here it came. I knew he'd ask me to pray for his wife, and I also knew that after I prayed for her, she'd still be blind.

But he let me off the hook. "You can see my wife is blind," he said. "She has been blind for nearly six years now. When you think about this happy old couple down here in Greenville, pray that God will let her see well enough to do her housework and watch the grandbabies grow up."

With that, they turned and started back up the aisle. I heaved a sigh of relief, even as I felt more than a twinge of guilt over my lack of faith.

It wasn't until about a year and a half later that I was back in Greenville for another concert. Again, the church was packed, and I didn't see my old friends until after the service when I looked up and saw them making their way toward me. She was still holding his arm, and I wondered how to start the conversation.

Perhaps something such as, "Well, I see you're still blind."

I needn't have worried because she took control of things. She leaned over and took a hymnal out of the rack, thumbing through it until she came to number 270.

"I've got the words memorized, but let me read them to you," she said.

And then she read:

"Amazing grace, how sweet the sound that saved a wretch like me. I once was lost, but now I'm found, was blind but now I see."

She looked up and smiled.

"I know that's spiritual," she continued, "but as you may remember, I was physically blind, but now I see!"

Then she pointed to her left eye. "Of course, this eye isn't quite as good as my right eye."

As they turned to leave, I heard a still, small voice whisper, "Oh, ye of little faith."

Like I said, I'll never figure God out! All I know is that what he plans is best for all his children. And because of that, there is hope. Because God is there, and because he loves his children so much, we can walk constantly in the light of his love, even if the journey should take us "through the valley of the shadow of death."

Is the Father Still There?

Do not let your hearts be troubled. Trust in God; trust also in me.

John 14:1 NIV

Doug:

The phone call from the doctor six hundred miles away brought the news that we were the grandparents of a boy with Down's syndrome—a boy who was fighting to hold on to life, a boy, we were told, who in all probability would never walk or talk.

And with that phone call, our lights went out. Was the Father still there? Did he care? Why did this happen to us? We were numb as we stumbled through the day. It was Wednesday and a well-known musical group was scheduled to perform at our church's midweek service. We went with our broken hearts, hoping that something would be said or sung that would begin the healing process. Just one word of comfort would have meant so much—one word that would have helped us to understand that God was looking down on us in mercy, that he understood and cared.

But it didn't come.

The members of the group did a superlative job on the catchy new tunes that made up the evening's repertoire. Their humor was quick and sharp, and people laughed. But we went home in the dark, still wondering if God was there. I was feeling angry and frustrated.

Then a memory came flooding back. It had to do with the release of my previous album. There had been a big party in the studio to introduce the new tunes to the Benson sales people and other guests from within the industry.

I remember saying to my accompanist as we walked into the party, "Let's just have fun. All these people know the Lord, and they'll really love the new tunes."

I felt great about what went on that day. I was in good voice and my humor was working. I met and shook hands with nearly everyone there and thought that, all in all, it was a grand release party.

One of the part-time sales people I met that day was a young preacher who was working on a master's degree and pastoring a little country church, even as he also dabbled in sales. I didn't know what was going on in that young man's mind that day. I didn't know what he needed. I was just there to "have fun."

But later that night, when he got home, he parked his car, walked through the moonlight to the little horse barn that stood behind his house, and there he blew his brains out.

I had not even tried to turn on the light for that troubled soul, and I had failed miserably to convince him that the Father was still there.

I have never again gone out to "just have fun," nor do I ever assume that "all these people know the Lord."

Would that young man be alive today if I had been true to my calling? I'll never know.

I had not brought to that young preacher the hope he so desperately needed. Neither had the polished singing group brought hope to us that night. When we stand before people to represent the Lord, it's serious business because there are always broken hearts present.

Laura Lee:

The doctor's words coming over the telephone from New Jersey sounded unreal to our ears: "You have a Down's syndrome grandson, Mr. Oldham." Doug asked the few particulars there were to know, thanked the doctor, and replaced the receiver. We sat in stunned disbelief.

Maybe there was some mistake. There had to be a mix-up. It took a while, but we finally got up enough courage to call Karen, our daughter. Her grieving told us it was true.

I left the next morning from Ohio, driving alone and planning to stay for a while to do what I could to help out. I cried and prayed out loud a lot of the way there: "Change the facts, Lord. Intervene." I demanded, harangued, pleaded, cried, and wore myself out. About five hours down the road, near Wheeling, West Virginia, I pulled into a Shoney's restaurant for some lunch. I was very discouraged because there had been no response from the Lord.

The restaurant had booths in the center so you could see into the booth on the other side of you. I watched as a young blond boy with wavy hair, pale skin, and blue eyes came to clear off the table across from me. At first I didn't really notice anything unusual about him. And then it hit me. He had Down's syndrome.

He looked into my eyes for a long moment and then gave me the most angelic smile I have ever seen. My heart gave a lurch. I don't know if I even returned the smile. Quickly, he cleared the table and then was gone.

For the rest of that lunch break, I looked for him, but he never reappeared. For some reason, he had calmed the storm that had been raging within. I drove the rest of the day with more ease and more faith.

I spent that night in a hotel room and got to Karen's the next day. By then the anxiety and fear were back in command.

I decided to get groceries before going over to the hospital. I think I was trying to delay the inevitable. What would I say when I saw my daughter face-to-face? How would I feel when I saw that baby?

As I sat in my car in the parking lot with my heart in my throat, a young boy walked across the front window of the grocery store. I didn't think he could see me, but I had a good view of him. And do you know what? He turned, looked at me, and smiled the same sort of angelic smile as the boy in the restaurant, and he, too, was a "victim" of Down's syndrome.

I went into the store to get my groceries, looking for him as I did so, but he was nowhere to be found.

I felt much better, though, and I was ready to see Karen and little Nathan.

Nathan means "gift from God," and even in the sorrow of the moment, Buz and Karen had the faith to name their son Nathan.

And what helped me accept him as a gift from God were those two nearly grown boys who had smiled at me with a message straight from the heart of God. I hadn't thought he was listening to me, but obviously, I was wrong.

Ten years later, I'm convinced that he sent two of his angels to minister his love to me.

Oh, yes, I believe in angels. And I'll tell you something else. My grandson is just about as close to being an angel as it's possible for a flesh-and-blood boy to be.

He is ten as I write this. He's in public school, doing well enough to be there, which is a great victory. He is reading, has learned to swim, goes to gymnastics class, and there's more. He also plays baseball, sings, plays the drums, and prays the greatest prayers I've ever heard. He's a handsome little guy with blond hair and a big smile. Mostly his life is full of victories.

And you know, you learn a whole new set of expectations when you have a Down's syndrome child in the family. Nathan was such a frail little baby that we learned to be grateful for very small victories.

We were always in the emergency room with him when he was little because his tiny digestive system just would not work. When he was two months old, doctors performed a colostomy. Then when he was two, another surgery restored things to normal.

The first operation meant he would live. The second one made him normal. Both were victories.

Another problem he had when he was small was that his arms were weak and limp. He couldn't crawl because his arms wouldn't support his weight. But Buz and Karen learned how to massage and exercise him until, today, his arms have normal strength. That, too, was a victory.

Karen enrolled him in a wonderful Catholic school for disabled children when he was only a few weeks old. He graduated when he was five. Once, when he was about three and a half years old, Karen sent us one of his report cards. The teacher had written, "Nathan is doing well. He is improving greatly in the broad jump. He is now able to jump two and a half inches." We were thrilled by that accomplishment. It was cause for celebration.

It's just like any accomplishment. The size of the obstacle overcome is the point of pride—not how big the feat may sound to someone else. A two-and-a-half-inch broad jump was a very big deal for our Nathan, and so we rejoiced. We still do!

God's love toward us is "tough love." He can take our questions and our sorrows and prove to us as time goes on that he is our loving Father and he is there.

God, Palm Springs, and the Fall of PTL

Fear not, for I have redeemed you;
    I have summoned you by name; you are mine.
When you pass through the waters,
    I will be with you;
and when you pass through the rivers,
    they will not sweep over you.
When you walk through the fire,
    you will not be burned;
    the flames will not set you ablaze.

Isaiah 43:1–2 NIV

Laura Lee:

Doug and I have been sharing with you some of the most difficult times of our life together.

And certainly our list of heartbreaks wouldn't be complete without touching on the scandal that rocked the PTL television network. Doug and I loved PTL, just as we loved Jim and

Tammy Faye Bakker, and those were terrible days for both of us.

PTL was a Christian theme park in South Carolina headed by Jim and Tammy Faye Bakker that was rocked by scandal in the late 1980s. There were charges of sexual sin and the mismanagement of money. We were on staff there at the time. Doug was one of the cohosts on the TV show and worked in the record and music department. I was Tammy Faye's companion, or "bodyguard." My close friends laugh at that, but Tammy Faye is so little, I at least looked like protection.

People sometimes say to us, "Why were you involved in PTL?" Well, considering how it all turned out, that's a fair question and one that deserves an answer. All through the years that he traveled, Doug always said, "Christians need a place to go to relax. They need a place that's nice where they can be with other Christians—a place to play, to pray, to get counsel if they need it, to go to church if they desire." We even tried to develop the idea through the years by taking people on vacation with us. When Doug saw PTL he said, "This is it. This is the place I envisioned."

It was a wonderful place, full of caring people who did their work "as unto the Lord." The one sure way to get fired from PTL was to be rude to a guest. Everyone worked to make it a place where Christians could relax and recharge their spiritual batteries.

When it fell apart, we were as shocked as everyone else and didn't know what to think.

Following the revelation of scandal, we spent some time in Palm Springs with the Bakkers, just letting them know that we loved and cared for them and always would.

On one occasion I was with them in Palm Springs while Doug was back in South Carolina helping to keep the TV show going. The Bakkers had bought the old Florsheim estate, which was almost in downtown Palm Springs. It was a large estate, which covered probably half a block of land, was fenced and hedged all around, and contained lots of trees, including a small orange grove. It also had two houses and a bathhouse.

The main house was a sprawling Mexican hacienda with a red tile roof, white stucco walls, and big glass walls in front and in back of the living room. Free standing in this room was a large, white stucco fireplace, rounded, as an old Mexican fireplace would be. The pool was off this room, along with the bathhouse. On the other side was the orange grove and a stone path leading through it to a little guest house, a miniature hacienda with a porch stretching all along its front.

In that house was an eat-in kitchen, a living room, a bedroom, and a bath with a brass sink. The entire house was decorated in soft southwestern colors and furniture. I got to live in it, and every woman who ever "played house" as a little girl will know what a thrill it was. The bed, made of white pine with straight lines and a canopy, was in a room with glass doors that opened onto the porch. From the porch I could see the orange trees and the beautiful, rugged mountains beyond. It was an enchanting place of great beauty and tranquility, a good place to have been while the storm of scandal was raging.

And it was raging. From the porch of this little house, Jim Bakker made his TV speech resigning from PTL. And then, everything turned upside down. We were literally prisoners on this property because there were so many news people camped outside the gate that we couldn't go out. They even got a cherry picker and took pictures inside the living room through the glass doors. We tacked up sheets for protection. Tammy and I devised some ingenious ways to sneak out too, but Jim never did.

We would crouch and dart, hiding behind trees in the field behind us, and have a driver pick us up on the other block. Sometimes I would sit up front with the driver and we would cover up Tammy with a rug on the back floor in order to get through the gate without any reporters seeing us.

Tammy had lots of wigs and disguises, which helped in her quest to look like anybody but herself. One day she overdid it, though, and ended up looking a great deal like Tina Turner, so we still had a crowd of people around us.

We lived through the resignation, the revelations about Jessica Hahn, the money scandals—all of it.

Doug would call from PTL with one set of facts, the local newspaper would give another set of facts, and the evening newscast still another. After a while, my mind and emotions went into overload. I was sure every day that I wasn't going to be able to take another day of this. But somehow, I managed to hold on.

At the same time, Doug and I had a personal upheaval of our own. A friend was going to leave us a small trust fund, which, given the circumstances, we were going to need. It was looking more and more like that was going to fall through. I had to leave in the middle of the PTL craziness to fly back to Ohio for her funeral. And then another friend, our best friend really, called to say she was leaving her husband. We were devastated by the news. In many ways, it seemed like our whole world was falling apart.

And so at night, all alone in this darling little house, I would pray and think, pray and think, trying to figure it all out. Usually I ended up exhausted, telling the Lord I didn't have a clue about what was going on, but that I'd leave it all up to him, and then I'd get some sleep.

Well, several mornings in a row, something wonderful and otherworldly happened—something special from God—reminding me that he was still in charge and that the universe was still operating under the banner of his love, whether or not I was able to feel it at the moment.

One morning, coming out of a deep sleep, I heard a deep, beautiful, male voice singing, "I will take care of you." My mind quickly corrected the lyric, silently reminding the unseen singer that the words to the song are "*God* will take care of you." But then the still, small voice within corrected my mind with "*I* will take care of you!" By this time I was fully awake and filled with a feeling of well-being and a sense of being loved—the peace that passes all understanding. This heavenly message was repeated three or four mornings in a row.

Searching the Bible for some understanding of this gift from the Lord, I found the most astounding verse.

In the Book of Zephaniah are these wonderful words: "The LORD your God is with you, he is mighty to save. He will take great delight in you, he will quiet you with his love, he will rejoice over you with singing" (Zeph. 3:17 NIV).

Isn't that amazing? God sings! He sings over *us*—with rejoicing!

He did, indeed, take care of us in special ways through all the PTL upheaval. He gave us unusual protection, he taught us to hold steady, not to run but to walk under his direction one day at a time. It was a scary time, but God was faithful to us.

One instance of God's faithfulness occurred on the day of the big auction when many of the things that became part of a media frenzy were to be sold. Doug said, "I dread going to the auction. There will be dozens of reporters all looking for staff people to interview. If I say the wrong thing, it could mean trouble for other people." Well, he had to go, so he dressed in white shorts, white sneakers, and a bright teal shirt. You could see him coming a long way off.

The reporters all knew us because they had set up camp on our front lawn. We lived by the Bakkers so from our property they could catch anyone coming and going from the Bakkers' house. At one point it was so hectic we moved out and went to a hotel. So the reporters knew Doug by sight.

The day of the auction, Doug walked around from 10:00 A.M. to 8:00 P.M. and not one reporter saw him. One time he was sitting right behind our daughter Dee at a display table and a reporter that we knew walked up to Dee and said, "I've been looking for your dad. Is he around here?" God made Doug "invisible" to reporters that day.

Many other small miracles happened—enough that we learned to lean on the Lord and not on our own understanding. So even though it was a sad time, a time that hurt many people, we were protected and given the chance to learn that on Christ the solid rock we can stand.

His message is true—totally true—and it applies to all his children. He says to all of us, "I will take care of you."

I had received another taste of his constant care during an earlier visit to Palm Springs, at another time when our lives were at low ebb and we needed something from God to keep us going. This time we were recuperating in another house that belonged to the Bakkers. Really, we were surrounded by luxury, but that sort of thing doesn't matter at all when you're feeling a poverty of the spirit, and we were. We had both had major surgery, with the result that we were in pain, physically and emotionally. And so the Bakkers, bless them, had decided that if we were going to be laid up for a while, we might as well be in pleasant surroundings, so they had sent us to their house in California.

The house where we were staying was the one the Bakkers had owned before they had sold it and bought the Florsheim estate. The house had a high wall around the front, and one a little lower in the back by the pool so you could look out onto the California desert. It was a very sleek, modern house, and perfectly furnished.

The front yard was landscaped with a small stream, a bridge, and a fountain. Whenever anyone came to the house, he or she rang the bell at the outside gate—a tall, completely closed, wooden gate. We could not see who was beyond the gate or the wall until we had gone outside to let them in.

Doug and I were a sorry lot, or as his dad would say, "a sad kettle of fish," because we were both almost completely out of commission. The sleek furniture was a nightmare. The couches and chairs had no arms, so Doug wasn't able to get in or out of them, due to being weak from his surgery. In desperation, we finally brought a lawn chair into the house.

The beds were the ones without bedsteads, with the tightly fitted bedspreads that had to be tucked in. To make them, we had to lift the mattresses all the way around as we went. With my insides cut and stitched the way they were, that was impossible for me to do. The car was so small and compact, it felt like we were putting it on to wear, instead of getting into it.

With all the surrounding glamour, we were still as sick, miserable, and lonesome as I ever remember us being in my entire life. The only two people we knew in Palm Springs were our two doctors. We were on the West Coast and all our family was on the East Coast. We even slept in different bedrooms, trying not to bother each other's fragile conditions.

One day I got to fretting about earthquakes, so I asked Doug if he had ever felt one.

He nodded, "Yes. One time when we were out here on a concert tour we had a small one."

My eyes widened. "What does it feel like?"

In typical male fashion he responded, "Oh, you'll know it when it happens."

"Oh."

Well, that night—sometime around 3:00 in the morning—I woke up, hearing what sounded like thousands of bowling balls coming down from the mountains. Then they hit the house, shaking everything, including me, with a quick, violent motion.

After that, the rumbling noise seemed to roll down the valley, just like it was some kind of giant bowling alley.

From his bedroom I heard Doug say, "Now *that* was an earthquake!"

From my bedroom I answered back, "I thought it was!"

Later on the news I heard that the quake measured five point something on the Richter scale. Now, in our weakened state, we had some cleaning up to do in this beautiful house.

Another thing about this house was that it had an elaborate alarm system for protection against intruders. Several nights around 2:00 or 3:00 in the morning the alarm had gone off. It seemed to be some type of malfunction, but as you can imagine, it unnerved us.

Actually, we did have one unexpected visitor. Every once in a while, a roadrunner would stroll down the patio between the house and the pool and peer in the glass doors as if to say, "Need anything today?" We loved him—our desert visitor. It was good to have any sort of company, although I certainly longed for the human kind.

One day I got up early and went out on the patio to read my Bible and pray. I was feeling particularly low and couldn't seem to shake the feeling that Doug and I were the only two people on the earth, so I finally prayed a silly prayer: "God," I prayed, "if you even know we're here, or care, send me some kind of a sign—a cactus that blooms unexpectedly, or something else that I'll recognize to let me know you're with me." Then I added, "I'm sorry for asking, but we're lonely here."

The day of the heat and sun and disability wore on. Then about 11:30 that night the doorbell rang out at the front gate.

I said in alarm, "We shouldn't answer it. Nobody knows us here, and that alarm's been going off every night. I'm scared."

Doug waved me off with a "Don't be silly" and struggled out the front door, over the bridge, past the fountain, to the huge closed gate. He opened it, while I stood at the door of the house, waiting for his return, my heart thudding away in my chest.

Suddenly, a great peal of familiar laughter rang out, along with Doug's exclamation of happy surprise. I wobbled out to behold a big, airport limousine whose driver was unloading the bags of our very precious visitor, the answer to my prayer, our daughter Dee. Her boss at PTL had told her, "Go take care of your folks for a week," and had handed her a ticket!

What a difference her presence made. After she came, everything exploded into life, activity, and laughter again. She bought groceries and fixed meals, rented videos to entertain us, and brought news and stories from home. We were connected to the real world again.

But the greatest part of all was that she arrived before midnight on the day I had asked the Lord to send a sign if he cared that we were dying of loneliness.

He cared. He *always* cares.

You can count on it!

Part Six

*Sweeter
As the Years
Go By*

Top: Laura Lee as a child, with her wagon
Middle: Laura Lee in front of the school she attended as a child
Bottom: Laura Lee and her cousins in front of the store in which they lived as children

All of This
and Grandchildren Too?

Gray hair is a crown of splendor;
it is attained by a righteous life.

Proverbs 16:31 NIV

Laura Lee:

Doug and I have been married now for forty-four years. Imagine that! And they said it wouldn't last. Shows you how much "they" know.

Even though our society seems to idolize the joys of youth, Doug and I can both tell you age has its rewards too. Not that we're old, you understand. We've just been around long enough to accumulate some of the better things of life.

Like grandchildren.

Jamaica was our first grandchild, and she got the attention and affection that such children usually get. Her dimple was firmly in place when she was a very tiny girl, bringing an extra glory to her infectious smile and laugh.

Jamaica is a beautiful teenager today, but one of my favorite memories of her has to do with the Christmas when she was turning three. (She was born on December 27.)

We lived in a grand old place, a house with a side entry that was actually a small room with a staircase going up from it to a big landing at the turn. Under the staircase were wooden seats that lifted up for storage. We had put Jamaica's little Victorian couch and chair in that area and used the storage seats for her toys. It made a perfect place for a child to play. In fact, the house was a marvelous place altogether for a child, with big porches, a fenced-in yard, and lots of animals roaming the property.

We had a great Christmas that year, with a big tree in the front entry. The tree was so big that it was almost too big, if you know what I mean.

Anyway, all the kids were home for Christmas, plus some of the young musicians from Doug's singing group. Doug's parents were also there, enjoying it all. I remember we had beef stroganoff for Christmas dinner because Doug's father, Papa Dale, was a big fan of stroganoff.

Someone had given me some expensive Godiva chocolates as a gift that year, but after the holiday I couldn't find them. Paula, Jamaica's mother, was there a lot, and although she kept helping me hunt for my candy, we never could find it. One day, in a fit of cleaning mania, we decided to clear out the old toys from those storage seats by the stairs to make room for the new ones that had been under the tree on Christmas morning.

We kept hauling things out and tossing them on the floor, and all at once I realized I was holding an elegant golden box—*the box*—my Godiva chocolates!

It had been safely hidden at the bottom of Jamaica's toy box.

I opened it and looked inside. Every chocolate had a tiny little nibble taken out of one corner—a minute sampling to determine the flavor of each confection.

Godivas, yet!

Little Jamaica, wee blessed child, stood rigid with a look of sheer terror on her tiny, white face. It was too much to bear. Paula and I began to laugh, and the more we laughed the funnier it got. Pretty soon the tears were rolling. Then we looked over at Jamaica who was acting like a little mechanical ballerina gone berserk! She was twirling and laughing and clapping her hands, curls bobbing, dimple dimpling, a perfect picture of sheer, unadulterated joy.

Why? She was forgiven. For some reason beyond her comprehension she was still loved in spite of what she had done.

She was experiencing the joy of the season, the same kind of joy we feel when we understand why the Christ child came—to bring us forgiveness for our transgressions.

I thought of that little incident recently when Jamaica was nominated, along with four of her girlfriends, for Fall Festival Queen at her high school. We were pretty excited, as you can imagine, and Doug and I went to the school chapel where the girls were presented to the student body and then were asked a series of questions, sort of Miss America style. I was so proud of Jamaica, who has grown into an innocent, exuberant, giggly, friendly, five-foot-tall, soft and curvy girl with long streaked blond hair. She still has the biggest dimple the Lord has ever bestowed on anyone's cheek.

After one rather knotty question, which Jamaica answered with a great deal of wisdom, I happened to glance back at her daddy, John, sitting in the back row. He was on his feet, giving his daughter a lone, long, standing ovation. How many troubled sixteen-year-old girls in our world today would give everything they own for a standing ovation from their fathers?

Anyway, we got to see all the girls and were very prejudiced in Jamaica's direction. We weren't sure whether she would win, though, because some of those other girls looked like models.

I think what pleased us most about the whole affair was Jamaica's thoroughly Christian attitude. She wanted to look good, of course, but she also wanted the other girls to look good, so she had a closet-raiding party at our house, looking for just the right "touches" to make her competition look their best.

The queen was going to be crowned during halftime of an important football game. Unfortunately for us, Doug and I had to be on the road and wouldn't be there for the big event, but we called home that day to tell her we would be praying for her.

Her response was, "Pray for my friends too. They're just as scared as I am." Good for you, Jamaica.

Later that night we called again to see what the outcome had been, and although Jamaica wasn't there, Dee told us with great excitement in her voice, "Jamaica won! She's the queen!"

We found out what time Jamaica would be home so we could call back to congratulate her. When we did, she answered the phone and Doug asked, "Is this the queen?"

"No, Granddaddy," she said. "This is Jamaica!"

They talked for a while and then Doug asked about her thirteen-year-old brother. "What did John do when it was announced that you were the winner?"

"Granddaddy, this is so funny. He jumped up from his seat in the stadium and yelled in a loud voice, 'We won! We won!'"

Doug and I sat in that motel room, miles from home, looked at each other and said, "*We* won!"

How is it that two very immature people, who started out limping along, flopping around, finally going down that well-traveled road of separation, headed for divorce, ever got turned around, straightened out, and set on the right path? How could we be sitting here forty years later saying, "We won"? How is it that we now have three wonderful grown daughters, all of them serving the Lord? How is it that we have two great sons-in-law, both model fathers, both in Christian service? How is it that we have four splendid grandchildren, all sweet Christians? We all like each other, we all get along, we all support each other. How did all this come about for a couple of poor little lambs who had lost their way?

I know the answer, and it lies within the blood of Jesus, the blood that was shed for you and me by God's wonderful grace.

God's grace has taken some very unusual forms through the years. Looking back we can see it, and with tears in our eyes, we can say with John, "We won! We won!"

Through the blood of Jesus "We have won."

John, Karen, John Jr., and Buz

Jamaica and her father, John, on the night she was crowned Fall Festival Queen

John Jr., Paula, and Jamaica

Paula

Karen

Dee

Jerry Falwell and Doug

Laura Lee and Doug

The Fortieth

Like a lily among thorns
is my darling among the maidens.

Song of Songs 2:2 NIV

Doug:

Forty years, and where did they go?

Our anniversary was coming on November 30th, and we knew it would be hard at that time of year to find the time to do anything special. We just had too many commitments throughout November and December.

But I wanted to do something special, something that would let Laura Lee know how much I love her.

Finally, I hit upon just the right idea. We would go, sometime in the middle of October, to visit the Colorado homestead where she had grown up, the place that held so many wonderful childhood memories, the place she had left when she was ten years old and had not been back to since.

I knew I had enough miles in my frequent flyer account to fly us both to Denver and back. We could rent a car there and spend a few days exploring all the old familiar places.

I figured we could also put in a stop in Canyon City, which is an hour or so from where the homestead had been. Laura Lee has a couple of cousins who live in the area, Bernice and Kenneth, and we were anxious to see them.

I was also looking forward to spending some time with Bernice's husband, Jack, who is a very accomplished musician. If it has strings, Jack can and does play it. He has even invented a couple of instruments, one of them being a double-necked guitar. I had only met Jack once or twice before and really liked him, so I was anxious to get acquainted with the entire family.

Laura Lee was also excited about seeing cousin Kenneth, who is about the same age as Laura Lee's brother, Glenn. She and Glenn had spent quite a bit of time playing with Kenneth when they were children, but she hadn't seen him for years.

Needless to say, Laura Lee was really looking forward to this trip—and so was I.

Finally, the big day came. We flew to Denver, rented our car, and started down to Canyon City. We drove past the impressive buildings of the Air Force Academy, past Steamboat Rocks, and finally into Colorado Springs. Laura Lee's mother had lived there for several years, so we drove past the house where she had lived and then on out toward Red Rocks to the big amphitheater where so many marvelous musical events are held.

It was dusk when we finally arrived in Canyon City, made a right-hand turn down the main drag, and saw the Royal Gorge sign that marked our hotel. The gorge itself was just a few miles north of us, and what a beautiful spot that was— such an impressive canyon, such rugged-looking country. It's easy to see why twenty-three movies have been filmed there. It was special for us to be in those surroundings.

That evening we visited with Jack and Bernice and had a wonderful time. Then the next day we went out to see the Royal Gorge. On our way we passed by dozens of deer. They seemed to be used to people, so we stopped and Laura Lee spent several minutes petting and feeding them. In case you haven't picked up on it by now, my wife has a great love for animals, and I'm pretty sure she could have stayed there all day with those deer.

But there was much to see, so I finally managed to pry her away from her four-footed friends, and we went on into the gorge itself. Somehow, and I don't really know how, I was even able to talk my hates-high-places wife into taking a cable car down to the bottom of the canyon. When we exited at the Colorado River and looked back up, we saw the bridge that carries traffic across the gorge, and my heart leapt into my throat. Was I actually going to drive across that bridge? I wasn't at all sure I wanted to.

For one thing, it was way, way up there. For another, it was made of wood, and you could see through the plankings. I didn't know if I'd be willing to put *my* weight on that thing, much less the weight of our car. But when I thought about it a little more, I realized that bridge has been carrying two lanes of traffic across the Royal Gorge for years so I finally figured it *must* be sturdier than it looked.

So when we got back to the top, we drove across, and then we stopped and walked back about halfway. We took pictures of a train rolling past in the valley far below, and of the mighty Colorado, rushing south in the direction of another breathtaking monument it has carved from God's earth— the Grand Canyon.

We had a wonderful dinner, including pan-fried trout, which I ate as often as I could on our trip, and then it was time to call it a day—a perfect day.

The next morning, I had (what else?) pan-fried trout for breakfast, and then, with Jack and Bernice joining us, we headed out in the direction of the old homestead, just outside the town of Hartsel. As we came down the road toward the little town, we could see it across the marsh, stretching along Route 24. A huge hotel had once stood in Hartsel, but it had burned down years ago and had never been rebuilt. At one time, people had flocked into the town to take advantage of the area's hot mineral water, and the hotel had done a brisk business. But that was many years ago.

The bathhouse that used to serve all those visitors was still there, standing on a peninsula that reaches into the marshlands where the hot springs have been flowing for hundreds of years. Steam still rose out of the marsh, and people still came to bathe in the waters, but the bathhouse had fallen into disrepair and many of the buildings in town were closed up.

This was where Laura Lee had come to shop with her parents when they lived on their homestead, and later on, she even lived near here for a while. She was sad to see what the years had done to the place.

We had to keep moving because it was almost time to meet Kenneth, who was to be our guide for the day. And what a day it was going to be!

Kenneth knew exactly how to get to the old homestead area, and it was a good thing, too, because there weren't any signs or other markers to identify it.

Nothing but thirty square miles of high plateau, where thirty families had once staked their dreams, put out their claims, and timbered the hillsides. They had pulled the logs down from the higher elevations, stripped and cut them on their own makeshift sawmills, and used them to build their homes, barns, and corrals.

But now we looked out across that high plane and saw nothing left of those thirty homes—nothing but one small shed standing in the middle of it all. There were no homes, no barns, no corrals—nothing at all to show that men and women had labored together here, had raised their families here, had given the land every bit of their energy and their devotion. I'm not sure, but I thought for a moment that I saw a tear in Laura Lee's eye as she looked out over the empty landscape that had once held all the bricks and mortar of her childhood.

Kenneth knew the area well, and he took us out and showed us where the old schoolhouse had been. We found some old timbers, but nothing else.

Laura remembered she had been to a dance at this schoolhouse when she was very small, no more than five, and a vicious fight had erupted. I guess when they fought out there on "the frontier," they really fought. Her mother tried to shield her, but Laura Lee was still hit in the face with spattered blood as the two men pounded away on each other.

That incident put a fear into Laura Lee's heart that has stayed with her, and standing there where the schoolhouse had been, the look on her face told me she was remembering the terrible incident in great detail.

An antelope ambled up to see what we were doing. He didn't want to get too close, but he didn't seem to be too frightened of us either. We unpacked our lunch and ate while Laura and the others talked about the days long gone. Even though I had been married to her for some forty years, I learned a lot about my wife and her people that day.

When lunch was over, we cut across the gentle slope toward the far side of the plateau, looking for Laura Lee's old home. Finally, Kenneth opened a wire gate, we drove through and turned right, went another half mile or so, and then stopped. There in front of us was the place of Laura Lee's beginnings.

An old well had been there, but it had been filled in to keep people from stumbling into it. We were also able to tell where the root cellar had been, and we found the place where the barn had stood. Lying on the ground was a very old bridle for a pony—probably one that had belonged to Laura Lee when she and Glenn were small.

We also found the hinges that had come from the barn door. Jack took them home with him, cleaned them up to get the rust off, repainted them black, and then gave them to Laura Lee as a souvenir of her childhood.

We went from the barn to where the house had stood. The spot was marked by heavy bottom timbers that had served as the foundation. They were rotting, but they were still there.

Laura Lee was so excited. She remembered that the piano had stood here as a kind of room divider, that a curtain had been here, her bed in this corner, and that she had been able to stand on the bed and look out the high window, seeing the majesty of Pike's Peak in the distance. She told us where the stove had been and showed us where she had taken her blanket and curled up in the mornings while the chill was being taken off the house by the big stove.

Memory after memory came flooding back. Beyond the timber where the front door had been, there had once existed a stone courtyard. The front yard had been marked on all three sides by stones, carefully laid out by hand. It was here that Laura Lee's mother grew flowers. This had been a special place indeed, built and cared for by wonderful people.

One of my prized possessions is a small snapshot of Laura Lee at age five, standing in front of a red wagon with a big farm dog sitting in it. Well, I don't know if it was red, really, because the photo is black and white—but what other color could a child's wagon possibly be? I was thrilled because as we walked through what had been the yard where Laura Lee had played as a child, we found that wagon. The wheels were gone and a tractor had smashed it flat, but it was her wagon, no doubt about it. We put it in the trunk of our car, along with the bridle and a few other souvenirs—including some ends of timber that still bore the notches Laura Lee's father had cut into them—and later shipped them home.

We spent a long day up there. I will have to admit that I hated to see it come to a close because it had brought me closer to my lovely Laura Lee's past. I knew a whole lot more about her father, her mother, and the other families that had dreamed their dreams up there on that high plane.

It was only because of her father's failing health that Laura Lee's family had left the homestead. When they did, they came back down to Hartsel where they helped to run a little grocery store, with one old-fashioned gasoline pump out front. The store and the pump were still there, but no trespassing signs and barbed wire warned visitors away, so we settled for some photos.

When we left the little grocery, we went out and found the sign that said "To Antero," and then we drove down and found the house where Laura Lee had lived while her daddy was caretaker and overseer of the Antero Reservoir. We crossed a little stream where Laura Lee and Bernice had looked for blue rocks when they were girls. Up the creek and over behind the grocery store was a bridge where Laura Lee and Bernice had hid one day so they wouldn't have to go to Vacation Bible School.

Laura Lee! Shame on you!

I didn't know it was possible, but seeing all her old places and hearing all her old stories made me love Laura Lee even more than I already did. And I was so glad that life eventually brought her to Anderson, Indiana, to attend college, and thus, into my life. Thinking back forty years, it had been a very good life.

We'd only been back home in Lynchburg for a few days when our package of treasures arrived. We were so excited as we opened it. There was the rusty wagon, smashed flat. There was the bridle and the pieces of rotting timber.

Finally, when it was all spread out in front of us, Paula, our oldest daughter, looked at our pile of treasure with a despairing, rather disgusted look and said, "You mean this is our inheritance? Don't you usually get money?"

She was joking, of course, but I've been thinking about that statement.

Yes, Paula, an inheritance usually is money. But in this situation, those timbers, notched by your grandfather, and that rusty old wagon, and those other things represent more than money. All those things are part of you—they go into the makeup of who you are.

You're fearless in the face of adversity, just like your grandpa. You're firm in your opinions about what is right and what is wrong, just like your grandma. You will tackle any project that needs to be done, no matter how big it is, just like both of your grandparents. You have an unfailing good humor and a streak of hilarity that is always breaking the surface, and in that way, too, you are very much like your grandfather.

You are real, honest, and fun, just like your wonderful sisters. And all three of you have inherited those traits and values from the two frontier people whose lives are represented in that rusty wagon and those notched log timbers.

I bless you, my precious daughters, and I honor your "inheritance."

Looking Back with Joy

You will grieve, but your grief will turn to joy.

John 16:20 NIV

Laura Lee:

It hasn't always been easy, this trek through life as Mrs. Doug Oldham.

I'd never tell you that I wouldn't change a minute of it. In the early days, there was plenty of grief and pain, and I'd certainly go back and change some of that if I could. But I know now that nobody's life is without its rainy days, and that God can take the rainiest of them and turn them into bright sunshine.

Looking back, I see many things, but most of all I see joy—deep, thankful joy that life has been, and continues to be, such a wonderful adventure.

For example, I remember the Christmas we spent in our marvelous house in Ohio. It was huge—twenty-two rooms, five fireplaces, seven staircases, two furnaces, two attics, two kitchens, fifty-two windows, and a porch seventy-two feet long with ten pillars.

How did we wind up with such a grand place? It all started because we couldn't afford furniture, so we began haunting used furniture places whenever we could. Pretty soon, we were hooked. We loved all the wonderful, sturdy old pieces that spoke of so much history and nostalgia. The oak furniture was cheap, solid, and fit our need for something that would last. I don't know, maybe we were looking for roots. Anyway, that's how the collection began.

Pretty soon we had so much that we needed a bigger house in which to store it all. Then an even bigger one. And finally, we had the house to end all houses.

It was in a little Ohio town, a block off the main street, and faced the Miami River, which is beautiful in the springtime. It was the most historical house in town, and we really couldn't afford it—but we loved it, and spent four years trying to put it all in order. We never completed the task, but we had an awful lot of fun trying.

That particular Christmas, the spirit of the holiday was really upon us, so we decided to put a candle in every one of our fifty-two windows. Of course, we didn't have fifty-two electrical outlets, so Doug bought a roll of electrical cord with little clamps, the kind that will let you connect the lights on one long cord running through all the rooms. He worked long and hard on it for most of the day, and finally they were lit.

When they were all glowing, it was a stirring sight. We went outside to admire the beauty of it all, and right on cue, it began to snow—big fluffy flakes. We went back inside and ate supper and then Doug suggested that we go for a walk in the snow.

"I'll take the camera and the tripod and we'll get some pictures with the candles in every window!"

It sounded like a wonderful idea to me, so we bundled up in our matching heavy-duty rough-out sheepskin coats.

Then we walked out into an enchanted land of lights and snow and old buildings in our quaint little town. Doug took pictures from every possible angle, and after that we walked a couple of blocks farther down and crossed the bridge so we could see how the house looked from across the river.

It was a sight to behold. It took my breath away. All around us the night was still and white and ethereal, and we were both reluctant to head back home. So, we walked slowly to a downtown cafe where the lonely meet for coffee and donuts. Doug and I watched and listened to "small town U.S.A.," which is, in itself, a unique experience. After sitting there for a while, nursing our after-dinner coffees, we buttoned up and walked back out into the still-falling snow.

We were about a half a block from home, in front of a closed storefront, when Doug stooped down to write in the snow.

I watched curiously as he knelt there for a few moments, but he was careful not to let me see what he was writing. Then he stood back up and gave me a secret little smile and a clear view of what he had written.

It read, "I love Laura."

When I read Doug's love note in the snow, a knot came into my throat and tears stung my eyes. I thought, "I'd gladly live another whole lifetime for a moment like this."

What if I had missed it by bailing out of the marriage thirty years ago? Some things are worth the work, worth whatever it takes to make them good. Marriage is one of those things, and I have never been more sure of it than I was the night I stood there looking at those words in the snow. "I love Laura." I knew that message would soon be covered with new-fallen snow. But it would remain forever in my heart.

May all women everywhere be so blessed.

In another time and another place, another man bent down to earth to write. He wrote, "I love you." But he wrote it not in snow, but in his own blood, for anyone who would be his beloved.

Thus, we are all blessed.

Before I get to the end of my story, I want to tell you about another occasion when God showed me his love in a special way and reminded me that no need ever escapes his notice. He also reminded me that nothing is lost that his love cannot restore, that nothing is endured that his love cannot make worthwhile.

It happened in Israel—God's beloved country. It was our first trip to the Holy Land, and we were all extremely excited. Through some wonderful good fortune, the whole family was able to make the trip. One of the big events of our lives happened there when Paula and John woke us up in the middle of the night to tell us they were engaged. What a wonderful memory that is.

The first night on the trip was spent in Amman, Jordan, and it was a rather nerve-racking experience because we were the first group of tourists to arrive in the country after a long ban on tourism had been lifted. Soldiers with guns watched our every move, and during the middle of the night we heard, for the first time, the Moslem muezzin and his eerie wail.

Because there were some problems having to do with our visas and reservations, it was a pretty long night for all of us. Doug was up well past midnight trying to get everyone settled.

Later on, as I was unpacking in our room, I discovered that my makeup kit was missing. It's a small case, easy to drop into my purse, but it wasn't there. In something of a panic, I took everything out of both the purse and my suitcase and laid it all out on the bed. No makeup kit. I went through it a second time. No doubt, I had lost it somewhere, and it wasn't like I could pop down to the nearest mall and buy a new one.

I know that's not an earth-shattering problem, but I was very embarrassed about having to show my naked face to all the people we were traveling with—and that included Jerry Falwell.

Later the next day, we arrived in Jerusalem, where we had made arrangements to have communion in the Upper

Room. There we experienced a time of worship that was truly extraordinary. We all felt the presence and power of the Spirit of the Lord more than at any other times in our lives. He was there with us, no doubt about it at all. Doug was leading us in the singing of some hymns, and he said later that he was literally afraid to start each new song, for fear it would somehow destroy the feeling of God's presence in that room.

I was sitting up on a narrow ledge with my purse just behind me. During this worship experience the tears were rolling, so I reached back without looking, and pulled my purse open to get a tissue.

I put my hand in the purse to feel around for one and, instead, felt something very familiar. It was the makeup kit that had not been there the night before, or in the morning when I was getting ready.

Chills ran over my whole body, and I prayed, "Lord, what are you saying to me?"

This thought came back instantly and plainly: "What you think is lost can be restored!"

"Lord," I cried out in my heart, "what is lost? Doug and I are together, we're well, the children are all here, and we're all saved. What is lost?"

The thought came back, "It's for the future."

The moment passed, and life went on. But then there was a moment, not so long ago, when I got terribly ill, so ill that it seemed doubtful I would recover. My life was hanging in the balance, but with God's help, I did slowly recover. I experienced Psalm 30:2–3: "O Lord my God, I called to you for help and you healed me. O Lord, you brought me up from the grave; you spared me from going down into the pit" (NIV).

As I was struggling to regain my health, it came to me one day as a flash of light.

"What you think is lost can be restored!" God is so good and faithful! I had thought my health was lost forever, but it was restored, and God had sent me a message years earlier through the small miracle of the makeup kit that it would be so.

I want to tell you again that there is hope—whatever storm you may be passing through. Be it ill health, financial difficulties, marital strife, loneliness, depression—whatever it may be—God loves you and he can bring you safely through.

Believe me. Whatever you think is lost can be restored. If anyone knows the truth of those words, it's me.

"I will restore to you the years that the locust hath eaten. ...And ye shall eat in plenty, and be satisfied, and praise the name of the LORD your God, that hath dealt wonderously with you" (Joel 2:25–26 NKJV).

Looking Ahead with Hope

I press on to take hold of that for which Christ Jesus took
hold of me.

Philippians 3:12 NIV

Doug:

If you'll bear with me, I want to tell you one more story.

Pastor Jim Burchett had just dismissed his midweek
prayer meeting, and the members of his congregation had
gone their separate ways.

It was a cold, rainy night with a piercing wind blowing in
from across the river.

In the cloakroom of the church, as Pastor Jim was getting
ready to leave, he almost bumped into a huddled figure—an
alcoholic who had slipped in out of the night seeking shelter.

The man looked out through eyes that were rimmed with red.

"Are you the preacher?" he asked in his thin voice.

Surprised, Pastor Jim nodded affirmatively.

"Preacher, can I stay in your church tonight? It's cold outside."

Pastor Jim looked at the man's thin, soiled clothing, his unshaven face, and pity stirred within.

But the fellow was a derelict. Let him stay and he'd probably steal the candlesticks or a typewriter, anything he could sell to get more liquor. So Pastor Jim said, "I'm sorry, friend. I'd like to let you stay, but I just can't."

The old man didn't seem surprised and turned to go. But as he did, Pastor Jim remembers, "It was just like a voice spoke to me saying, 'A cup of cold water in the Master's name.'"

"Wait a minute!" Pastor Jim called after the old man.

"If I let you stay, will you promise not to steal anything?"

There was a hesitation and a shuffling of feet. Then the derelict replied, "You mean you'd take the word of an alcoholic?"

"No," the pastor answered, "but I'd take the word of a man."

Tears came into the old fellow's eyes as he said, "Preacher, I promise." And then, because he knew himself so well, he added, "And I'll try to keep my promise."

Down in the church basement was a couch near the furnace room, so Jim found some quilts and a pillow that had been donated for missions and were awaiting shipment, made up the couch, and left with anxiety in his heart.

The next morning, when he returned early, the old man was gone. The quilt was neatly folded, with the pillow resting on top of it.

The old man, whose name was Charlie, stayed in the church basement several times that winter, and his visits gradually became more frequent as spring arrived. It was getting to the point where it was too much, and it had to stop.

"Charlie," said the preacher, "I sure hate to say it, but I can't let you go on like this."

Charlie nodded meekly. "I understand, Preacher."

But Pastor Jim had begun to like the old fellow, almost in spite of himself. One evening as they were making up the bed, he asked Charlie if he had ever wanted to be set free from his alcoholism.

Charlie looked shocked. "Are you kidding?" he asked. "Only every day of my life."

"Well, have you ever prayed about it?"

"Yes, I have, Preacher... but God doesn't hear the prayers of an alcoholic. He isn't interested in me."

That night Jim slept very little. Instead, he tossed and turned in his bed, praying for his new friend, a fellow human being who needed the help that can come only from God. The next morning he told Charlie that he had spent the night praying for him.

Charlie looked stunned and muttered, "Nobody's prayed for me in years."

The pastor was moved by that statement and asked, "Charlie, will you come into the sanctuary with me and let me pray for you?"

"Sure," came the answer, "but it won't do any good."

Despite Charlie's doubtful reluctance, the two of them went upstairs into the sanctuary, where they kneeled side by side. Pastor Jim poured his heart out to God, asking for a miracle.

As he prayed, the old man began to sob. Then softly spoken words were heard, mingling with the brokenness, as the old man confessed to the Lord a long list of the evils he had done and asked for forgiveness. For fifteen minutes or more he prayed. And then, when he had finished, he looked up with hope on his face.

"Preacher, I feel different."

Jim hoped it was so. He took Charlie out for breakfast, and then the old man went on his way.

The next Sunday morning, Pastor Jim was shocked and thrilled to see Charlie in church, sitting in the back pew. His clothes were washed, the ragged beard was gone. The old man sat there with a big grin on his face all during the service. Afterward he said, "Preacher, I know I don't belong here. I can't dress well enough to attend church, but I had to tell you that I haven't had a drop to drink since you prayed for me.

"I'm sober for the first time in fifteen years."

The pastor rejoiced with Charlie regarding his sobriety and assured him that he was dressed just fine. "We want you to come to church, Charlie."

Charlie took him at his word.

From that day forward, Charlie was in church any time the doors were open—Sunday morning, Sunday night, and Wednesday night.

But there was another problem. The old guy felt bad because he never had anything to put in the offering plate when it came his way.

Finally, he hit upon an idea.

Approaching the pastor after church one Sunday evening, he said, "Preacher, I really want to give something to the Lord. Will you let me take care of the church?"

Well, the church already had a custodian, but he didn't always open the church early enough for the convenience of the people. Sometimes they gathered out front before the door was unlocked. And Jim knew it would be a good thing to give Charlie some work to do. So he had a key made, gave it to Charlie, and told him he wanted him to be on hand to open the building an hour ahead of every service.

"Turn on the heat and the lights. And then when services are over, stay around until everyone is gone so you can turn everything off."

Charlie was delighted. "Thanks, Preacher," he said, as he put the key in his pocket. "Now I can do something for the Lord."

Charlie was faithful to his trust. For the next year, the doors were always open and the building was comfortably warm—or cool, in summer—when people arrived for each worship service. For the old man, it was a labor of love. He was so grateful for the way the Lord had changed his life—and in all that time, he never touched another drop of liquor.

And then one day Pastor Jim got a phone call from the local police.

"Do you know a man by the name of Charlie?"

"Yes, he's a friend of mine."

"Well, I regret to inform you that he is dead."

It turned out that Charlie had been walking down the street when he had a massive heart attack. He died instantly. When the police had come to the scene, they found in Charlie's pocket a note with Jim Burchett's phone number on it.

They asked Jim to come down and identify the body, which he did. Then they gave him Charlie's few possessions, among them the key to the church. Jim put it in his pocket and went to make arrangements for the funeral. He was sad to see Charlie go but thrilled at the same time because he knew that his old friend had entered into glory. His years of homelessness were truly over.

Charlie had gone home to be with Jesus, and the preacher wanted to give him a proper farewell. He told the undertaker, "Look, I know this is a county case and you won't make anything on it, but would you mind if we had the service in the church?"

The undertaker said that would be just fine.

Mrs. Burchett got on the phone and called around to make sure enough people showed up to make a respectable showing at the funeral.

Then the afternoon of the funeral, Jim had to make an emergency call at the hospital. When he finally got back to the church, it was exactly time for the service to start, but one look told him something was wrong. Why were all these people standing outside? Why was the casket still in the hearse?

The pastor went over and asked the undertaker what was going on.

He shrugged and said, "We can't get in. The door's locked."

The pastor's hand went into his pocket and came out with the key—Charlie's key. He took it and unlocked the door so the service could begin.

Charlie had done his work so well that everyone had taken him for granted. And so it was that Pastor Jim put his prepared notes aside that day and talked to the people straight from his heart. The story of Charlie had somehow given new meaning to the notion of giving a cup of cold water in the Master's name.

Well, Jim and his people have a beautiful new church on the corner now, and right near the front entrance, etched in a panel of glass, are the words: "In loving memory of Charles Alvin Skeens, who opened the door that others might come in."

I think about old Charlie a lot.

I think he understood the truth of these words: "Better is one day in your courts than a thousand elsewhere; I would rather be a doorkeeper in the house of my God than dwell in the tents of the wicked" (Ps. 84:10 NIV).

Charlie knew what it meant to be redeemed, and so do I. He knew what it meant to feel like a failure in life, and so do I—in fact, I doubt if anyone has ever felt like more of a failure than I did the day Laura Lee took the girls and left me.

But praise God, he allowed me to find my way back into his service, and I've spent my life trying to open doors for him so he could come in and do his work in people's hearts. My key has been my songs, my words, and, thanks to his grace, my marriage and my family, which is to say, my life.

I thank God and I thank Laura Lee for working so hard to fulfill the words of the old song—make something beautiful out of my life!

And, you know, even though I have walked very closely with God for more than thirty years now, I'm still learning more about him all the time and finding new reasons for falling in love with him.

For example, in October of 1993, a friend challenged me to pursue a newer, deeper relationship with God the Father and Jesus Christ the Son and my Redeemer. Both the Father and the Son have many more attributes than these, of course, but this is where my search began.

By September of 1994, my knowledge had greatly increased, but I had not found the relationship that I so earnestly desired. And then one day during early autumn, after I had spent the entire day in the Scriptures, I was sitting in the front room in the fading light of dusk. The house was quiet and no lights had been turned on.

I'll have to admit that I had been asking why my search for a closer relationship with the Father and his Son had taken so long and had not been more fruitful.

Suddenly, these words were imprinted on my mind: "I will be with you and will help carry the load." I didn't hear a voice, though the communication was indelibly etched in my mind and has dramatically changed my life. It was so real to me that I answered out loud, "Okay, I can live with that!" I directed my comment to an invisible presence across the room by a corner of the television set.

By the following day, which was Saturday, I had gotten up enough nerve to remind God that in his Word it says that he will not only be *with* his people, but also *in* them. I told him I wanted to experience that in a new way—I wanted him to sing *through* me the next day.

And he did. He was there in my music in a way I had never experienced him before. That marked the beginning of a new dimension in my music. Since that time, I have consistently asked him to select the songs for the Sunday TV programs and for our concerts. Almost always, by Wednesday morning I am impressed with the song for the 11:00 A.M. Sunday service. By Friday evening, I have been guided to the song for the 10:00 A.M. service.

On Sundays I go into the sanctuary for prayer no later than 6:30 A.M., and when we are doing concerts, Laura Lee and I like to spend at least an hour beforehand praying for God's blessings.

The old tensions are gone, and I find myself looking forward, more than I ever did before, to sharing the love of God with the people he chooses to have in the audience.

And so, as Laura Lee and I come to the end of this time of sharing with you, I want you to know that there really is hope. If life is stormy all around you right now, don't give up! God loves you! He wants to carry you through!

You know, the old song is really true. Life can be "sweeter as the years go by." I know that's true because I have experienced it for myself.

My love for Laura Lee is sweeter.

My love for God is sweeter.

My love of music is sweeter.

All of life is sweeter.

My prayer for you is that God will grant the same for you, that your life, too, truly will be sweeter as the years go by.

Epilogue

Top: Laura Lee with a shepherd boy in Israel
Middle: Doug and Laura Lee in Jerusalem
Bottom: Doug at the Sea of Galilee

Epilogue

The Peace of Jerusalem

Peace I leave with you; my peace I give you.

John 14:27 NIV

Laura Lee:

We were back in Israel for the fourth time, a little older and a little less sure whether we could keep up with a tour group.

The first day scared us terribly. It was September and the weather should have been nice, but as the guide explained, the area was experiencing an "unusual weather pattern." In actuality, that meant it was hotter than it had been in fifty years at that time of year. There were also winds—dry, hot winds—like the Santa Ana winds that wreak so much havoc during fire season in Southern California.

Our guide was small, dark, sturdy, and obviously used to walking. His stroll was our trot, and his brisk walk was our run. Our first stop was the old walled city where we were going to walk the Via Dolorosa, the Way of the Cross.

The walk began uphill and was always and forever after that uphill. There were steps every few feet—each one a challenge to Doug—and the whole walk was on crowded, narrow streets, some of which were entirely closed overhead so no sunlight came through. It was unbearably hot and oppressive, and the smell of rotting garbage was overwhelming. The shops were open and the crowds were dense—jostling, noisy, and all foreign to us. We had been warned about pickpockets, unscrupulous merchants, and beggars, and we saw them all.

Try as we might, we were always at the tail end of our group, and I was worried about Doug, who was drenched with sweat, breathing hard, and certainly not having fun.

But then, fun is not what the Via Dolorosa is all about. It is, instead, about the supreme sacrifice made by our Lord Jesus, who also struggled to walk these hilly streets. He, too, was jostled by the crowd—a most hostile crowd. He smelled the rancid smells, he sweated, and he stumbled and fell under the weight of the burden he was carrying—a mean and heavy cross, and the mean and heavy sins of the entire world.

Once in a while, someone would try to reach him, to help him, to bless him. He knew who and was grateful.

But he also knew that ultimately the burden was his and his alone to carry.

After walking along that same path on that unbearably hot autumn afternoon, I had a renewed understanding and empathy for what our Lord went through. When we finished our walk and were finally back on our bus, I thought, "I never want to see the 'old city' again."

Well, a few days went by and our tour director, Carlene Westover, said, "I have a friend in the old city who has a jewelry shop. We're getting a few people together, hiring a taxi, and going later tonight so we can shop without a crowd. Do you want to go?"

Well, now! Shopping, you say? Of course, it was too tempting, so we said we'd go, even though I felt afraid of the old city streets and the uphill walk, and at night, yet. But still, a shopping trip like that seemed very much worth the challenge, so when supper was finished that night, we got our group together, found a taxi, and took off.

When we arrived in Old Jerusalem, our host met us at the Jaffa Gate to walk with us to his shop. After about half a block, we left behind us all the people, all the noise, and all the lights of our twentieth-century civilization. The shops were closed, and no one was around except for one or two shop owners who were cleaning up after a long day.

After walking a couple of blocks, we made a turn onto a broad street where vaulted Roman pillars supported rooms and apartments built over the street. The only light was three blocks down, dimly illuminating the sign of our host's store. Then we sensed something otherworldly.

As we walked slowly and casually toward the light, it was as if the very air were suddenly suffused with peace, with an unseen glory. I couldn't believe it, and neither could Doug. It was the same place all right. The smells were still there, the steps were still there, but now there was a calmness, a sweetness, a soft glow, accompanied by a total and complete absence of fear.

We shopped for a long time, buying Christmas gifts for our kids, and came out after 11:00, when the shop owner walked with us back to the Jaffa Gate.

The same sense of peace and luminous glory was in the air.

We walked back a different way, by a fountain in an open circular area, where we could see the sky and the stars shining brightly above us.

We stopped and immersed ourselves in the night and in the beauty of the feeling of the glory of the Lord. Doug looked at me with wonder on his face and said, with awe in his voice, "They may have torn his house down, but he's still here."

I have never heard a truer statement. When God said he would live in Jerusalem, he meant it. The Wailing Wall and some recent excavations are all that's left of the temple, his house. But no matter what men can and will do to it, Jerusalem is still "The Holy City." And when the harsh crowds are absent, you feel only one thing—his peace.

John 20:19 says, "On the evening of that first day of the week, . . . Jesus came and stood among them and said, 'Peace be with you!'" (NIV).

Notice that the Scripture says "Jesus came and stood among them." He came to them. He still comes to us today in varied and wonderful *personal* ways. We have been pleased to share with you the ways that he has come to us in our lives.

So as long as Jesus comes and stands and lives among us and dwells in us, in the Holy Spirit, there is peace—peace as real as the peace of a Jerusalem night. And there is hope! As long as there is Jesus, there is hope!

Doug Oldham has traveled 2.5 million miles and has given more than five thousand concerts in the past thirty-five years. He has appeared in Billy Graham Crusades, has been the featured soloist on the *Old Time Gospel Hour*, and has co-hosted the *PTL* club. He has given concerts around the world, including appearances before five United States presidents and the Queen of England and stops at Wolftrap, Carnegie Hall, and the Pontiac Super Dome. His sixty-four albums have sold millions of copies.

Laura Lee Oldham is a writer and motivational speaker. She assists Doug in his musical concerts and is also busy speaking to women's groups and churches across the country.

For both Doug and Laura Lee, their family has been their top priority despite their busy schedules. They have three daughters and four grandchildren.